B

Nonfiction Strategies for Reading Results

Authors

Leslie W. Crawford, Ed.D.
Professor of Literacy
Georgia College & State University

Charles E. Martin, Ph.D.
Professor of Early Childhood and Middle Grades Education
Georgia College & State University

Margaret M. Philbin, Ed.D.
Associate Professor Emerita
State University of New York Potsdam

Vocabulary and Fluency Consultant

Timothy V. Rasinski, Ph.D.
Professor of Education
Kent State University

English Language Learner Specialist

Caroline Teresa Linse, Ed.D.
Fulbright Scholar
Minsk State Linguistic University
Minsk, Belarus

Zaner-Bloser

Photo Credits

Covers: (flying bat) FPG International; (girl with batteries) Herral Long, Photographer; (volcano eruption) Telegraph Colour Library/FPG International; (Martian landscape) Courtesy of NASA; (kids on train) Hulton Getty/Tony Stone Images; (Nevelson sculpture) National Institute of Health.

Models: George C. Anderson Photography

pp. 3, 68(R), 73(B), Peter Gridley; pp 4, 8, 10(R), 81(R), 105, Telegraph Colour Library/FPG International; pp. 5, 177, Ken Frick/Image State; pp. 10(L), 13(I), 14, Stephen Dalton/Animals,Animals/EarthScenes; pp. 9 (L), 22(L), 27, OSF/A. Bannister/Animals,Animals/ EarthScenes; p. 9(R), Beverly Factor/Image State; p. 11, Planet Earth Pictures/FPG International; pp. 13, 152, 160, 178, FPG International; p. 16, Doug Wechsler/ Animals,Animals/EarthScenes; p. 17, Richard Sheill/Animals,Animals/EarthScenes; pp. 22(R), 25, McDonald Wildlife Photography/Animals,Animals/EarthScenes; p. 23, Carlos Dominguez/CORBIS; p. 26(T), William Dow/CORBIS; p. 26(B), ROYALTY-FREE/ CORBIS; p. 28, Sheldan Collins/CORBIS; pp. 32(L), 36, Paul A. Zahl/Photo Researchers, Inc; pp. 32(R), 34, Scott Johnson/Animals,Animals/EarthScenes; p. 33, Norbert Wu/NSF Oasis Project; p. 37, Peter Davis/Photo Researchers, Inc; pp. 45(L), 58(both), 59, 60, 62, 63, Herral Long, Photographer; pp. 45(R), 69, Paul Seheult; Eye Ubiquitous/CORBIS; pp. 73(Top, both), 135, Zaner-Bloser, Inc.; pp. 80, 82(L), 83, Paul & Lindamarie Ambrose/Getty Images; pp. 81(L), 94(R), 95, 98, Elliott Smith/Image State; pp. 82(R), 86, 87, Warren Faidley/Image State; p. 88, Dennis Fisher/Image State; pp. 104(R), 107(B), Robert Reiff/Getty Images; pp. 104(L), 109, Alan Kearney/Getty Images; p. 107(T), Earl Kogler/Image State; p. 108, Hilary Wilkes/Image State; pp. 116, 117(both), 118(both), 119, 120, 122, 123, 130(both), 132, 133, 136, 140(both), 141, 143(both), 144, 145, Courtesy of NASA; p. 131, Garry Buss/FPG International; pp. 153(L), 166(L), 169, Hulton Getty/Tony Stone Images; pp. 153(R), 176(R), 179, Historical Archive/Getty Images; pp. 154(L), 158, FPG Historical Collection; pp. 154(R), 161, Frank Cezus/Getty Images; p. 155, Bruce Roberts/Photo Researchers Inc.; pp. 157, 180(L), Getty Images; p. 159, Union Pacific Museum Collection; p. 167, Kansas State Historical Society, Topeka Kansas; pp. 176(L), 181, Andre Jenny/Image State; p. 180(T), Archive Photos; p. 180(R), Image State; pp. 188, 195, Normand Maxon, New York Public Library; pp. 189(L), 202, 206(both), Harper Collins; pp. 189(R), 210(R), 215, National Institute of Health; pp. 190(L), 194, Eva F. Maze; pp. 190(R), 196, Jack Mitchell; p. 203, HWR Productions; p. 211, Tony Vaccaro/Archive Photos.

Art Credits

pp. 44, 46(both), 47, 48, 50-52, Stephen Marchesi; pp. 49, Richard Loehle; pp. 68(L), 69-72, Ron Himler; pp. 94(L), 97, Joe LeMonnier; pp. 166(R), 172, Holly Sierra; pp. 191, 193, From *Alvin Ailey* by Andrea Davis Pinkney, illustrated by Brian Pinkney. Text © 1993 by Andrea Davis Pinkney. Illustration © 1993 by Brian Pinkney. Reprinted by permission of Hyperion Books for Children, an imprint of Disney Children's Book Group, LLC.; pp. 204 HarperCollins; pp. 210(L), 212-214, Diana Magnuson.

ISBN 0-7367-2352-8

Copyright © 2005 Zaner-Bloser, Inc.

Zaner-Bloser, Inc., P.O. Box 16764, Columbus, Ohio 43216-6764 (1-800-421-3018)

Printed in the United States of America

05 06 07 08 (106) 5 4 3

Table of Contents

Table of Contents (continued)

Hi! We're your
READ FOR REAL
Reading Team Partners!

Have you noticed that the reading you do in science and social studies is different from reading stories and novels? Reading nonfiction <u>is</u> different. When you read nonfiction, you learn new information. We'll introduce you to some strategies that will help you read and understand nonfiction.

In each unit, you'll learn three strategies—one to use **Before** you read, one to use **During** your reading, and one to use **After** you read. You'll work with these strategies in all three reading selections in each unit.

In the first selection, you'll **Learn** the unit strategies. When you see a red button like this ◉, read "My Thinking" notes to see how one of us used the strategy.

In the second selection in each unit, you'll **Practice** the strategies by jotting down your own notes about how you used the same unit strategies. The red button ◉ will tell you where to stop and think about the strategies.

When you read the last selection in each unit, you'll **Apply** the strategies. You'll decide when to stop and take notes as you read.

Strategies

Here they are—the **Before, During,** and **After** Reading Strategies.

Use these strategies with all your nonfiction reading—social studies and science textbooks, magazine and newspaper articles, Web sites, and more.

	BEFORE READING	DURING READING	AFTER READING
UNIT 1	**Preview the Selection** by looking at the title and headings to predict what the selection will be about.	**Make Connections** by relating information that I already know about the subject to what I'm reading.	**Recall** by summarizing the selection in writing or out loud.
UNIT 2	**Activate Prior Knowledge** by looking at the title, headings, pictures, and graphics to decide what I know about this topic.	**Interact With Text** by identifying the main idea and supporting details.	**Evaluate** by searching the selection to determine how the author used evidence to reach conclusions.
UNIT 3	**Set a Purpose** by using the title and headings to write questions that I can answer while I am reading.	**Clarify Understanding** by using photographs, charts, and other graphics to help me understand what I'm reading.	**Respond** by drawing logical conclusions about the topic.
UNIT 4	**Preview the Selection** by looking at the photographs, illustrations, captions, and graphics to predict what the selection will be about.	**Make Connections** by comparing my experiences with what I'm reading.	**Recall** by using the headings to question myself about what I read.
UNIT 5	**Activate Prior Knowledge** by reading the introduction and/or summary to decide what I know about this topic.	**Interact With Text** by identifying how the text is organized.	**Evaluate** by forming a judgment about whether the selection was objective or biased.
UNIT 6	**Set a Purpose** by skimming the selection to decide what I want to know about this subject.	**Clarify Understanding** by deciding whether the information I'm reading is fact or opinion.	**Respond** by forming my own opinion about what I've read.

Now that you've met the team, it's time to get started.

Unit 1

Strategies

BEFORE READING

Preview the Selection

by looking at the title and headings to predict what the selection will be about.

DURING READING

Make Connections

by relating information that I already know about the subject to what I'm reading.

AFTER READING

Recall

by summarizing the selection in writing or out loud.

LEARN
the *strategies*
in the selection
All About Bats
page 11

PRACTICE
the **strategies**
in the selection
The Scoop on Scorpions
page 23

APPLY
the strategies
in the selection
Deep-Sea Dangler
page 33

Think About
the
Strategies

Preview the Selection
by looking at the title and headings to predict what the selection will be about.

My Thinking
The strategy says to preview the selection by looking at the title and headings to predict what the selection will be about. The title is "All About Bats." I looked at the headings, and they all refer to something about bats. I predict that this selection will tell about different kinds of bats and how bats are helpful. Now I'm ready to read and see if I'm right.

Make Connections
by relating information that I already know about the subject to what I'm reading.

My Thinking
The strategy says to make connections by relating information that I already know about the subject to what I am reading. I will stop and think about this strategy every time I come to a red button like this ⦿.

All About Bats

Flying foxes (megabats) at dusk

What flies like a bird, can see with its ears, has fur like a mouse, and works nights? It's a bat! Bats fly through the night using sound to find their way. During the day, they hide in trees and caves with their wings folded neatly.

You may hear people say things about bats that may or may not be true. You may hear that bats are blind. And they suck blood from animals, including humans. You may hear that they will get tangled in your hair. What IS true about bats?

What Is a Bat?

Bats are mammals. Mammals are animals that have hair. They give birth to live babies. They feed milk to their young. Bats meet all of those requirements, so they are mammals. So are dogs, gerbils, antelopes, and humans.

Bats are the only mammals that can fly. Some other mammals, such as flying squirrels, can glide. But only bats can truly fly. They use wings just as birds do. Birds' wings are covered with feathers. Birds have strong chest muscles to move their wings with enough force for flight. But bat wings are made of two thin layers of skin. The skin stretches between their finger bones at the top. It attaches to their ankles at the bottom.

Bats feed at night. Have you ever tried to walk through your house in the dark? If so, you know that seeing is not as useful in the dark as it is in the daytime. Bats are **nocturnal** animals. Nocturnal animals are active at night instead of during the day.

Anatomy of a Bat

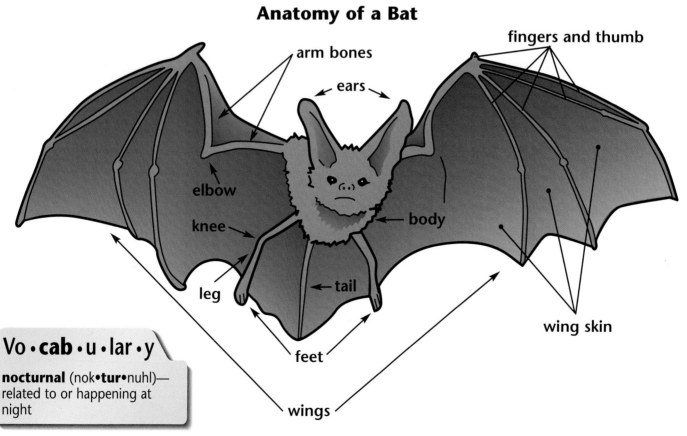

arm bones

fingers and thumb

ears

elbow

knee

body

leg

tail

feet

wing skin

wings

Vo • **cab** • u • lar • y

nocturnal (nok•**tur**•nuhl)— related to or happening at night

[12]

Free-tailed bats (microbats) leaving a cave in Carlsbad, New Mexico

Megabats and Microbats

Bats are found all over the world. There are many different types. They are usually placed in one of two groups: the **megabats** or the **microbats**.

The prefix *mega-* means "large." But megabats are large only when compared with microbats. They weigh from three to four pounds. They have wingspans of up to six feet. Megabats are sometimes called flying foxes. Their furry bodies, pointed noses, and large ears remind people of foxes. The straw-colored flying fox is an example of a megabat.

Megabats live mostly in Asia and in Central and South America. They feast on the plants that grow all year round in hot, humid climates near Earth's equator. They eat fruits, **nectar,** and pollen.

Micro- means "small." Microbats usually weigh less than two ounces. Two common microbats are the big brown bat and the silver-haired bat. The smallest microbat is called the bumblebee bat. It lives in Thailand. This bat is about the size of a jellybean. It weighs less than a penny.

Vo•cab•u•lar•y

megabats (meg•uh•bats)— bat species that eat mainly fruits and nectar, may grow to four pounds, may have wingspans of six feet, and live in Asia and in Central and South America

microbats (my•kroh•bats)— bat species that eat mostly insects and may weigh less than two ounces

nectar (nek•turh)—sweet liquid produced by plants

All of the bat species that live in North America are microbats. But microbat species are found all around the world. They live in caves, in attics, and under **eaves** of buildings. They may live under loose bark on tree trunks. These are places where it is safe during the daytime, when the bats sleep. Some bats are colored to look just like dead leaves. They hang from trees to rest.

Strategy

Make Connections by relating information that I already know about the subject to what I'm reading.

My Thinking

I never thought about bats around my house or hanging from tree branches and looking like leaves. I really do need to learn more about bats!

Vo·cab·u·lar·y

eaves (eevz)—the over-hanging parts of a roof

Bats at rest

Most bats hang upside down while sleeping and resting. When they are ready to fly, they just relax their toes and off they go—into the night for a delicious meal of mosquitoes, moths, and other insects. Most microbats eat insects—lots and lots of insects. Other microbats eat fish, birds, and frogs.

Three species of microbats feed on blood. They're called vampire bats. But they don't suck blood like vampires in a horror movie do. Instead, they make a tiny break in an animal's skin. Their meal is the blood that flows out of the wound. None of the vampire bats feed on human blood. All three species live in Central or South America.

How Bats Use Sound

Most bats have good eyesight. To get around in the dark, though, they use their voices and ears in a special way. Bats make very high-pitched sounds through their mouths or noses. The sounds travel out from the bat until they hit something, like a yummy mosquito! The sounds bounce off the mosquito. They travel back to the bat's large ears. The bat is able to tell the mosquito's location from the strength and direction of the echo. The bat's sending and receiving of sound waves is called **echolocation**. Echolocation uses a bouncing sound wave (echo) to find (locate) something.

Bats are experts at echolocation. They can tell a mosquito from a bit of paper in the dark. They can keep from hitting each other or running into buildings, trees, and wires. So they can also keep from getting tangled in a person's hair. It is extremely rare for a bat to touch people. Their echolocation skills keep them (and your hair) safe.

How Bats Are Helpful

Bats are important to the health of the places where they live. They keep insect pests under control by eating tons of insects every night. The bats that feed on nectar and pollen help spread pollen from plant to plant. That's how plant eggs are fertilized to form seeds and fruits.

Strategy

Make Connections by relating information that I already know about the subject to what I'm reading.

My Thinking
I've heard about bats getting tangled up in people's hair, but I didn't know this isn't really true.

Vo•cab•u•lar•y

echolocation
(ek•oh•loh•**kay**•shuhn)—
a system of senses in which highpitched sounds are sent out and their echoes tell the animal where and how far away something is

Bats that feed on fruits spread seeds for those plants. They usually squeeze the juice out of a fruit, swallow the juice, and then spit out the seeds.

Bats rarely have contact with humans. They use echolocation to avoid humans. Any time a bat will let you get close enough to touch it, it is probably sick. That is why you should never touch a bat or other wild animal. It may carry rabies or another disease. In the United States, rabies from any source is extremely rare (fewer than 30 cases in the past 25 years). Only a small number of cases have ever been caused by bats.

These short-nosed fruit bats help with the pollination of fruit trees.

People are the main threat to bats. They fear bats and believe things about bats that aren't true. People may destroy bats and places where they live. People should learn how bats help them, not hurt them. Then maybe they'll try to protect bat caves and other places where bats live.

A Bat Invitation

Invite bats to live in your neighborhood. You can get instructions for how to build a bat house from the natural resources department of your state. You'll need a hammer, a saw, nails, some scrap lumber, and a ruler. Hang the bat house. Encourage bats to feast on the mosquitoes that want to feast on you! As you learn more about bats, you'll be glad to have them in the neighborhood.

A bat house in winter

Think About the Strategy

AFTER READING

Recall
by summarizing the selection in writing or out loud.

My Thinking
The strategy says I should recall by summarizing what I've read. I can do this by telling the main parts of what I read.

I learned that bats are mammals that fly and hunt at night. There are two main types of bats, mega-bats and microbats. Bats eat mostly fruit, bugs, pollen, and nectar. They hardly ever hurt people.

Bats are really good neighbors because they cut down on bug pests and they help plants make fruit and new plants.

Graphic organizers help us organize information. I think this article can be organized by using a spider map. Here is how I organized the information. I put my central idea in the middle. I used main ideas for the legs of the spider. I put details about the ideas on the lines coming out from the legs.

Spider Map

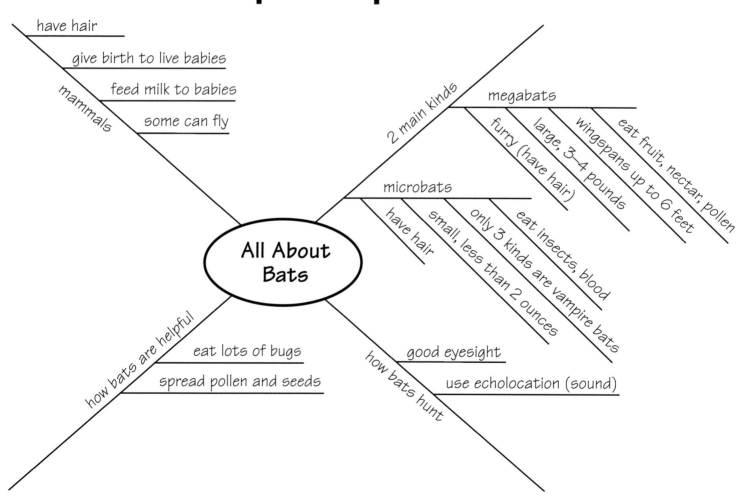

All About Bats

mammals
- have hair
- give birth to live babies
- feed milk to babies
- some can fly

2 main kinds

megabats
- furry (have hair)
- large, 3–4 pounds
- wingspans up to 6 feet
- eat fruit, nectar, pollen

microbats
- have hair
- small, less than 2 ounces
- only 3 kinds are vampire bats
- eat insects, blood

how bats are helpful
- eat lots of bugs
- spread pollen and seeds

how bats hunt
- good eyesight
- use echolocation (sound)

I used my graphic organizer to write a summary of the article. Can you find the information in my summary that came from my spider map?

A Summary of
All About Bats

Many people are afraid of bats. They have heard scary stories about them. Here is the truth: bats are mammals, like us. They have live babies and feed milk to their babies, like us. However, bats can fly. They are the only mammals that can fly.

There are two kinds of bats: megabats and microbats. Megabats are bigger. They weigh three to four pounds. Megabats are furry and look like flying foxes. They live mostly in Asia and in Central and South America. Microbats weigh less than two ounces. They live all over the world. The bats in North America are all microbats.

Megabats eat fruit and the nectar and pollen from flowers. Microbats eat lots and lots of insects. Some microbats eat blood from animals! They are called vampire bats.

How do microbats hunt down all those insects? During the day, they can see well. During the night, they use echolocation. They send out high-pitched sounds. These sounds bounce off any insects near-by. The sounds travel back to the bats, like an echo. Then the bats know where to find the insects.

Bats are helpful. Many bats eat bugs, especially mosquitoes. Some bats spread pollen from plant to plant. Then the plants can grow seeds and fruits.

Bats are really very interesting little animals. When you know the truth about bats, they aren't scary at all!

Introduction
Here is my introduction. It tells what I will write about. The main idea is in the center of my spider map.

Body
I used information from each leg of the spider map for each paragraph in my body copy.

Conclusion
I summarized my paper by recalling the main ideas.

Prefixes

Sometimes a word part can give you a good clue about a word's meaning. A **prefix** is a word part at the beginning of a root word. The prefix can change the meaning of the word. The prefix *mega-* at the beginning of a word means "large." Here is an example of a word with that prefix from "All About Bats":

megabats, which means "large bats"

Here are other *mega-* words with their meanings:

megahit—a big hit
megaphone—a device for making the voice sound larger
megavitamin—a large dose of vitamin

The prefix *micro-* at the beginning of a word means "small." Here is an example of a word with that prefix from "All About Bats":

microbats, which means "small bats"

Here are other *micro-* words and their meanings:

microscope—an instrument that makes small things look bigger
microcomputer—a very small computer
microbe—a germ too small to be seen without a microscope

On your own paper, write each word and then match it with its meaning. Use the word part after *micro-* or *mega-* to help. Use a dictionary if you need more help.

1. microclimate

a. a very large, tall building

2. microdot

b. a tool for measuring very small distances

3. micrometer

c. the climate of a small area

4. megastructure

d. one million dollars

5. megascopic

e. an image that has been reduce to a very small size

6. megabuck

f. large enough to be seen by the naked eye

Readers' Theater

Here is a conversation between two microbats. A narrator helps set the scene. With other students, practice reading the script aloud until you can read it with expression. When you are ready, present it to an audience.

Fluency TIP

Remember that exclamation marks show that a word or phrase should be read with more emphasis and enthusiasm than other words.

All About Bats

Narrator: Fred and Dana, two microbats, hang out together. They live in the eaves of a cozy old barn in some New Hampshire woods. One summer evening, at dusk, Dana is poking her friend with her wing. She wants him to wake up.

Dana: Come on, Fred. It's time to get up.

Fred: Go away, Dana! I'd rather sleep.

Dana: Sleep! What are you talking about? I'm hungry, and the mosquitoes out there sound fat and tasty.

Fred: Mosquitoes! I don't think there are any left.

Dana: What are you talking about?

Fred: Don't you remember? You said that if I wanted to get as big as my hero, Manny the Megabat, I'd have to eat every mosquito in New Hampshire. Well, last night I flew around like crazy, and I think I ate them.

Dana: (Trying to hold back her laughter) Oh no, I was only kidding. Fred, you weigh about two ounces. Manny the Master Megabat weighs four pounds! You could never get that big.

Narrator: Poor Fred rubbed his belly, which was still as big as a walnut.

Fred: No?

Dana: No. That would be like a human who likes elephants trying to eat every hamburger in Ohio!

Fred: The human could never get as big as an elephant—even with all the milkshakes in Minnesota! Or every turnip in Texas!

Narrator: Fred was on a roll now, and Dana's sides were splitting from laughing so hard.

Dana: Or how about all the ice cream in the world?

Fred: Ugh! That makes me sick—thinking of someone eating ice cream.

Dana: Yeah, I know. Or milkshakes! That's so sickening!

Fred: You're right. Let's go get some yummy moths!

Dana: That sounds delicious. Maybe we can find a caterpillar for dessert!

Think About
the Strategies

BEFORE READING

Preview the Selection
by looking at the title and headings to predict what the selection will be about.

 Write notes on your own paper to tell how you used this strategy.

DURING READING

Make Connections
by relating information that I already know about the subject to what I'm reading.

 When you come to a red button like this ●, write notes on your own paper to tell how you used this strategy.

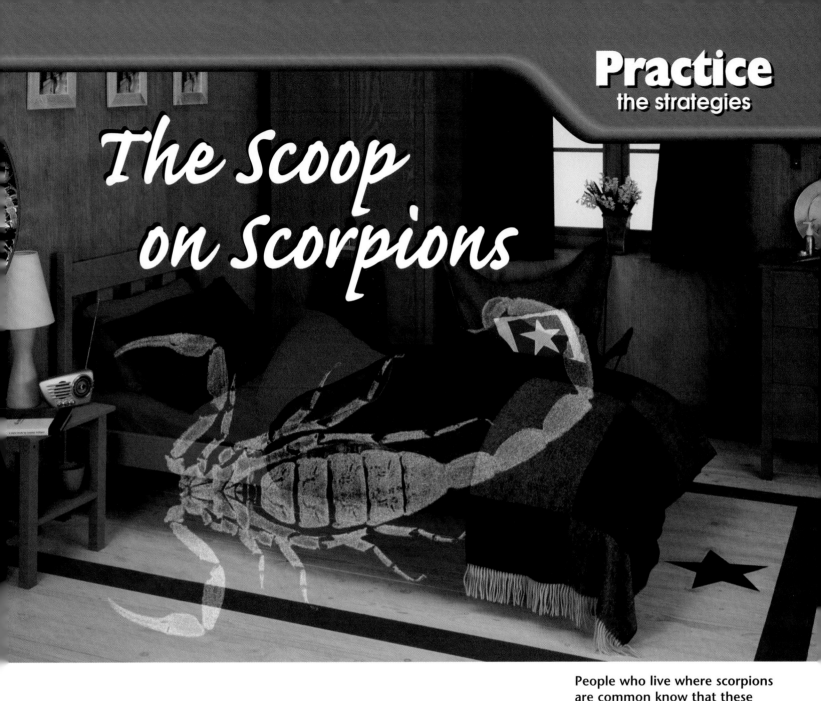

The Scoop on Scorpions

People who live where scorpions are common know that these animals like to hide in warm, dark places.

Many people live in parts of the country where there are scorpions. Scorpions like to hide in dark places. It is dark inside your shoes and your slippers. It's also dark under your bed covers. What would you do if you found a scorpion hiding in your room?

You may know that scorpions can sting. But did you know they are in the same animal family as spiders and ticks? And did you know that scorpions really prefer to hide than to fight with you? Read on to learn more of the scoop on scorpions.

What Is a Scorpion?

Scorpions are small nocturnal animals. They have claws like lobsters. They sting with their tails. Their bodies, including their tails, are divided into eight parts called **segments**. Scorpions look like lobsters for a good reason. They are in the same family, or group, as lobsters. They are **arthropods**. Spiders are arthropods, too. Unlike insects, which have six legs, spiders have eight legs. Like scorpions, they may bite. The bodies of arthropods are covered with a hard outer shell for protection.

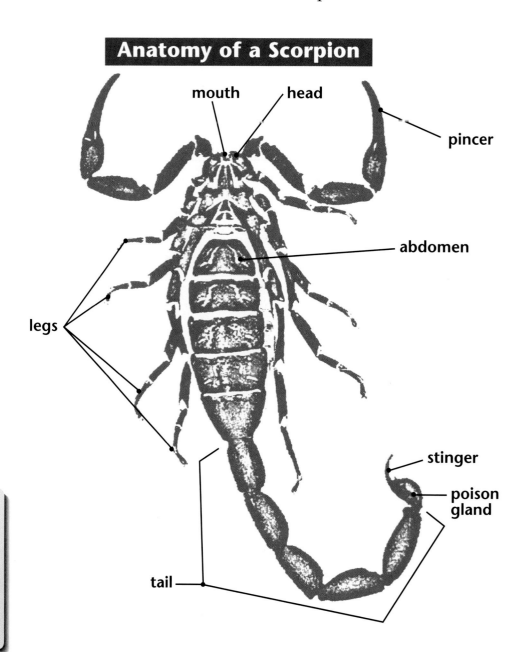

Anatomy of a Scorpion

mouth   head

pincer

abdomen

legs

stinger

poison gland

tail

There are about 2,500 species of scorpions. They live in warm places, like deserts. But they are also found in many other **habitats**. Other scorpions live in places such as rain forests, caves, along the shore, and on mountains.

Most scorpions are small. They are less than 2 inches long. The smallest scorpions are less than ⅕ inch long. The longest scorpions grow to be 8 inches long. Scientists have found fossils of ancient scorpions that were longer than 16 inches. There have been scorpions before, during, and after the time when dinosaurs lived. They are good **survivors**.

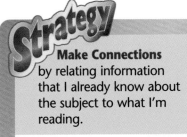

Strategy

Make Connections by relating information that I already know about the subject to what I'm reading.

Write notes on your own paper to tell how you used this strategy.

The Scorpion Polka

Scorpions have an unusual mating dance. The male grabs the claws of the female. Next, they dance around in a sort of scorpion polka. At last, they find just the right spot for mating. Scorpions give birth to live babies. This is unusual among arthropods. Most arthropod babies hatch from eggs. Actually, scorpion babies hatch from eggs, too, but they hatch inside the mother. Then the young are born alive. A mother scorpion takes very good care of her babies. They often hitch a ride on her back.

A mother scorpion with her babies

Vo·cab·u·lar·y

habitats (hab·i·tats)—the places where something naturally grows and lives

survivors (suhr·vy·vuhrz)—ones that stay alive

[25]

Make Connections
by relating information that I already know about the subject to what I'm reading.

Write notes on your own paper to tell how you used this strategy.

Big Claws, Little Claws

The biggest scorpions are not necessarily the most dangerous. Danger depends on the type of **venom** the scorpion has. Venom is the poison that scorpions and some other animals use to kill their food and to protect themselves. Most scorpions are harmless. They may pinch you or sting you. But the pinch will be small. The sting will not be worse than a bee sting.

Some scorpions do have venom that is so strong that it can kill a human being. The only deadly species is the sculptured scorpion. It lives in the United States. Its **range** is from Mexico up into Arizona and southern Utah.

Scientists have found that **pincer** (or claw) size is a good way to tell how poisonous a scorpion is. Scorpions with stronger venom depend less on their claws. Their claws tend to be smaller. Scorpions with weaker venom depend more on their claws. Their claws tend to be larger.

The scorpion above was photographed under "night light." Notice the size of the pincers on these two scorpions.

Vo·cab·u·lar·y

venom (**ven**•uhm)—a kind of poison some animals have, usually spread during a sting or bite

range (raynj)—the area in which something happens or where an animal lives

pincer (**pin**•suhr)—a special claw that can grasp and hold something

Food Comes to the Scorpion

In the desert, food is hard to find. Scorpions are very slow animals. They try to use as little energy as possible in catching their food. Although they like to eat, they can get by for more than a year without food.

A scorpion makes its desert home under a rock. It stays there during the hottest part of the day. At dusk, the scorpion and most other animals in the desert come out. The scorpion finds a good spot to wait for its **prey**—maybe a juicy spider—to come by. The scorpion stays very still until the spider is close. Then it uses its claws to grab and hold the spider while it kills it with its **fangs**. Only if the prey is large does the scorpion sting it with its tail. Stinging takes too much energy.

Strategy

Make Connections by relating information that I already know about the subject to what I'm reading.

Write notes on your own paper to tell how you used this strategy.

A scorpion eating a desert grasshopper

Vo·cab·u·lar·y

prey (pray)—an animal that is hunted or caught for food

fangs (fangz)—special tooth-like structures the scorpion uses to bite its prey

Scorpions are **nearsighted**. In the daytime, they can hardly see. But their vision is perfectly suited for the darkness. They see best just when their food is most active. Scorpions seldom drink. They get most of their liquids from the moisture in their food, such as the grasshopper pictured on page 27.

Not all scorpions live in desert areas. This scorpion is hiding under a large leaf in a tropical area. Notice the size of its claws.

Shake Your Shoes

If you live in the southwestern United States or in Mexico, you probably know how to stay safe around scorpions. You shake your shoes before you put them on. You check under your blankets before you go to bed. Scorpions that are trapped indoors seek out these dark spots. They resemble the homes scorpions naturally choose out in the desert. If you do get stung, tell an adult. If the symptoms seem worse than a bee sting, you may need to see a doctor.

Vo•**cab**•u•lar•y

nearsighted (**neer**•sy•tid)—not able to see things at a distance clearly

Scorpions are an important part of the food chain where they live. In that way, they help the **ecosystem**. They are food for owls, lizards, mice, bats, and sometimes even other scorpions. Scorpions are shy. If you leave them alone, they will not hurt you.

Vo·cab·u·lar·y

ecosystem
(ek·oh·sis·tuhm)—all the various parts of an animal's environment

Think About the Strategy

AFTER READING

Recall
by summarizing the selection in writing or out loud.

Write notes on your own paper to tell how you used this strategy.

Vocabulary

Context Clues

Sometimes an author's words can help you figure out the meaning of a new word. The author adds **context clues** by giving examples for the word. Often, the words *like, as, also,* and *such as* tell you that the author is giving you an example and that example is a context clue.

Read this paragraph from "The Scoop on Scorpions":

> *There are about 2,500 species of scorpions. They live in warm places, like deserts. But they are also found in many other habitats. Other scorpions live in places such as rain forests, caves, along the shore, and on mountains.*

How can you figure out the meaning of *habitats?* Look for the clue words *like, as, also,* and *such as.* Look for context clues, or examples of the word. Examples here include *deserts, rain forests, caves,* and *mountains.* The text says, "They live in warm places, like deserts. But they are **also** found in many other habitats." *Also* is another clue that a habitat is a place where scorpions live. So now you know that *habitats* are places where animals live.

Read this excerpt from the top of page 28 in the article "The Scoop on Scorpions." Use context clues to figure out the meaning of *moisture.* Look for examples of the word. Also look for the clue words *like, as, also,* or *such as.*

> *Scorpions seldom drink. They get most of their liquids from the **moisture** in their food, such as the grasshopper pictured on page 27.*

On a separate sheet of paper, write a definition for *moisture.* Explain how clue words helped you.

Poetry

In this playful poem, a scorpion named Scoop plays with his cousin, a lobster. Read the poem several times aloud to yourself until you think you can read it with good expression and appropriate phrasing. You may want to read it with a partner so that you alternate lines or stanzas.

TIP

Poems should be read with good phrasing and a sense of rhythm. As you practice this poem out loud, try to capture in your reading the rhythm that makes the poem flow.

Scoop Scorpion

Scoop Scorpion and Lobster Boy
set out one hot, hot day.
Said Scoop to cousin Lobster Boy,
"We arthropods need to play!"

Lobster Boy took off for shore,
while Scoop did claw and climb
the tallest mountain south of here.
His tempo was slow time.

Now scorpion got hot that day
from too much desert sun.
He liked to hide beneath a rock
until the day was done.

This desert heat was way too much
for scorpion to take.
But Lobster Boy ran off to swim
and left poor Scoop to bake.

Think About
the
Strategies

BEFORE READING

Preview the Selection
by looking at the title and headings to predict what the selection will be about.

DURING READING

Make Connections
by relating information that I already know about the subject to what I'm reading.

AFTER READING

Recall
by summarizing the selection in writing or out loud.

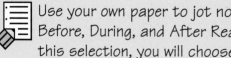 Use your own paper to jot notes to apply these Before, During, and After Reading Strategies. In this selection, you will choose when to stop, think, and respond.

Deep-Sea Dangler

Giant clams, tube worms, and crabs live deep in the ocean.

Imagine the darkest darkness, the coldest cold. Think of something pressing down on you. It presses so hard that you may be crushed. But look! Off in the distance, there is a light, a tiny dot of white. It acts as a **beacon**. It is drawing you forward. You go toward the light. Suddenly you are pulled forward into the belly of a huge beast! What is this beast? Is it fact? Is it fiction? It's fiction if you're a person. It's fact if you're a fish living deep down in the ocean.

It's Fact

The creature **luring** you out of the dark with its light is called an anglerfish. It lives deep in the ocean where no light can reach. Light from the sun can reach down to only about 3,000 feet below the ocean's surface. Below that point, it is always dark. This is the home of the anglerfish. And there are more than 200 kinds of them!

Vo•cab•u•lar•y

beacon (bee•kuhn)—a signal fire or light

luring—pulling you into a trap

[33]

A deep-sea anglerfish

The Fishing Fish

Angler means "someone who fishes." An anglerfish, like a human angler, dangles bait in the water. All 200 kinds of anglerfish use their "bait" to attract prey. The anglerfish above has a fin on its back that sticks out like a fishing rod. The tip of the rod glows. This is an exciting sight in the darkness. The light attracts other fish. Slowly, the anglerfish pulls the bait, and its dinner, closer to its mouth. Then it opens its huge jaw. Water rushes into the anglerfish's mouth. The prey animal is caught up in the **current**. It ends up right in the anglerfish's stomach!

Dinner in the Deep

All the food in the deep ocean comes from above. No plants can grow where there is no sunlight. This means that deep-sea fish are in one of two groups. They are **predators,** which catch and eat other animals. Or they are **scavengers,** which eat dead matter that drifts down from high up in the ocean. The scavengers are eaten by predators, which in turn eat each other. Some fish feed

Vo•cab•u•lar•y

current (**kur**•uhnt)—moving water in a larger body of water

predators (**pred**•uh•tuhrz)—animals that live by hunting and eating other animals

scavengers (**skav**•uhn•juhrz)—animals that live by eating dead or decaying matter

[34]

near the surface at night. But they spend the day in the **depths**. They are eaten by fish like the anglerfish, which stay below 3,000 feet all the time. Either way, the food comes from the part of the ocean where sunlight reaches and plants can live.

Anglerfish have huge jaws compared with the rest of their bodies. If you were an anglerfish, your mouth and jaw would take up almost your entire head! Why do so many deep-sea fish have huge mouths? Well, food is so scarce that a fish can't let any food go by—even food that seems too big. Some fish mouths are lined with teeth that slant backward. Dinner can't get back out once it is caught! Many of these fish have stomachs that stretch, too. The fish may also use the currents caused when they open their mouths. The currents pull in their prey. They don't have to use energy chasing their food. The anglerfish, in fact, is a very slow fish. It rests in the water, dangling its light. The curious fish drawn by the light do all the work.

Ocean Depths

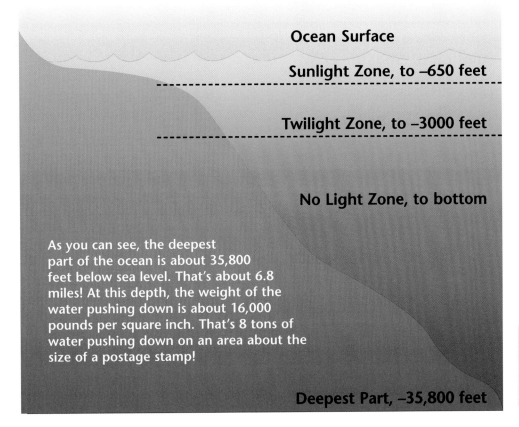

Ocean Surface

Sunlight Zone, to –650 feet

Twilight Zone, to –3000 feet

No Light Zone, to bottom

As you can see, the deepest part of the ocean is about 35,800 feet below sea level. That's about 6.8 miles! At this depth, the weight of the water pushing down is about 16,000 pounds per square inch. That's 8 tons of water pushing down on an area about the size of a postage stamp!

Deepest Part, –35,800 feet

Vo·**cab**·u·lar·y

depths—deep places in a body of water

Glowing From Within

Many sea animals glow. In fact, below 6,000 feet, most animals glow in some way. The anglerfish dangles its light. The lanternfish has glowing lights under its eyes. They beam like a flashlight. The viperfish has a row of lights inside its mouth. Other fish come to check out these lights. Then the viperfish just closes its mouth, a well-lit trap. Living things that glow are **bioluminescent**. *Bio-* means "life," and *luminescent* means "producing light."

A saber-toothed viperfish

Bioluminescent light is cold light. It isn't like electric light, which makes light and heat. In bioluminescence, four **substances** work to make light with no heat. Some animals, such as fireflies, make the substances in their bodies. They make their own light. Other animals, such as most of the bioluminescent fish, farm the work out. The dangling light of the anglerfish, for example, is caused by glowing bacteria. The fish supplies food to the bacteria. The bacteria glow for the fish.

A glowing (bioluminescent) anglerfish

Anglerfish Life Cycle

An anglerfish lays her eggs deep down in the ocean. They float to the surface. In time, they hatch. That's the last light the anglerfish will see. As they grow, they drift downward. By the time they are young adults, they are **submerged** in darkness.

Female anglerfish grow 8 to 12 inches in length. Some species grow as long as 40 inches. Only female anglerfish glow. Male anglerfish are small compared with the females. In most of the 200 kinds of anglerfish, the males attach to the side of the female. In the deep darkness, this is a way for the fish to make sure they will always have a mate. The female does the fishing and eating for both of them. The male gets food from the female's blood.

It's Fiction

The scene in the first paragraph is fiction for you. You, a person, will never be threatened by an anglerfish. For one thing, the weight of the water is great. At 3,000 feet below the surface, where the anglerfish live, the water is so heavy a person would be crushed. For another thing, you are a lot bigger than an anglerfish. Thank goodness! Let's keep fish that eat humans where they belong—in books and movies.

Vo·cab·u·lar·y

submerged (suhb•murjd)— covered with water

Vocabulary

Multiple Meanings

Many words have more than one meaning. You can understand the correct meaning by seeing how the word is used in the selection. For example, reread this passage from "Deep-Sea Dangler":

Water rushes into the anglerfish's mouth. The prey animal is caught up in the **current**.

The word *current* has more than one meaning. It can mean:

- happening at this moment
- moving water within a larger body of water

How can you tell which meaning fits this passage? The passage is about what happens underwater. So the meaning for *current* in this passage is the second definition, "moving water within a larger body of water." When you know multiple meanings for words, you can avoid confusion when you read.

On a separate sheet of paper, write sentences that show you understand at least two different meanings for each of these words. Use a dictionary if you need help.

1. page	**6.** hand
2. face	**7.** foot
3. spring	**8.** run
4. trim	**9.** back
5. bat	**10.** leg

Poetry

This poem is about how an anglerfish uses its own light to attract its dinner. Practice the poem several times until you think you can read or say it smoothly to an audience. You might present it with a partner, taking turns saying the chorus and the verses.

Poems should be read with good phrasing and a sense of rhythm. As you practice this poem, try to make the poem flow, much as a song flows.

The Anglerfish Song

Chorus   Angler
dangler
bangles
and beam.

Verse   Down in the deep, deep dark,
Down in the deepest sea,
Anglerfish dangle their light,
Bright for their prey to see.

Chorus   Angler
dangler
bangles
and beam.

Verse   Swim and swim to the light.
Light is bright and clear
Down in the deep, dark sea.
Anglerfish dangle right here!

Verse   Snap!
Anglerfish grabs that swimmer!
The big jaw opens wide,
And prey becomes good dinner!

Chorus   Angler
dangler
bangles
and beam.

Circle Graphs

How Many Mammals Are Bats?

Bats are mammals. People are, too. About 4,000 species (kinds) of mammals live on Earth. Of these 4,000 species, 1,000 are bats! This circle graph shows how many mammals are bats.

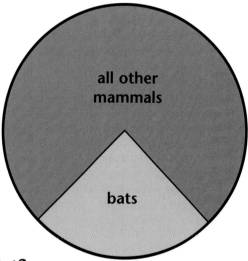

What Do Bats Eat?

Most bats eat insects. Some eat fruit and nectar. A few bats eat fish and small animals. Three kinds of bats drink the blood of animals. This circle graph shows how many bats eat each kind of food.

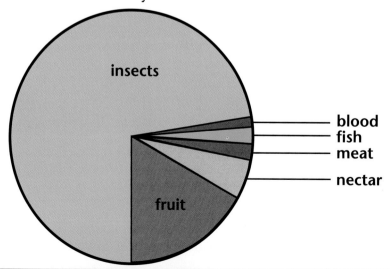

Discussion Questions

Answer these questions with a partner or on a separate sheet of paper.

1. What does the top graph show?
   a. Most of the mammals on Earth are bats.
   b. Most of the bats on Earth are mammals.
   c. One of every four kinds of mammals is a bat.
   d. One of every four kinds of bats is a mammal.

2. In the top graph, where would people be?

3. Look at the bottom graph. What does the "insects" part show?
   a. There are many insects on Earth.
   b. Most bats eat insects.
   c. Some bats eat fruit.
   d. Bats help us by eating insects.

4. Look at the bottom graph. What do the smallest number of bats eat?

5. What does the bottom graph tell you about the bats near your home?

6. After people use sprays to kill mosquitoes, what happens to bats?
   a. The bats have an easier time catching the mosquitoes.
   b. The bats find something else to eat.
   c. The bats start drinking blood.
   d. The bats go hungry.

7. How could your community attract more bats?
   a. Spray to kill the mosquitoes.
   b. Do not spray to kill the mosquitoes.
   c. Plant fruit trees.
   d. Plant more flowers.

8. Mosquitoes can carry diseases, such as the West Nile virus. Should communities spray to kill mosquitoes? Explain your answer.

EXPLORE MORE

Make a Display

Prepare a visual display of information about bats. This might be of one bat, showing its physical characteristics. Or it might be of several bats, comparing and contrasting their physical characteristics, habits, and habitats.

Make a Diorama

Build a diorama to display the special habitat of one of the animals presented in this unit.

Write a Play

Write a short play about a family that lives where scorpions are common. Have the characters talk about what they do when they find a scorpion in the house. Include tips on how they make visitors feel safe there.

Compare Bats and Scorpions

Develop a visual presentation of a bat and a scorpion. Compare and contrast the physical characteristics of the mammal and the arthropod.

Write a Report

Research and write a report on other animals that depend on bioluminescence as part of their life and survival.

Write Diary Entries

Imagine that you are on an expedition that is traveling to the deepest part of the ocean. Write diary entries for at least three days. Describe what you see outside the porthole and what you hear from the underwater microphone. Tell how the increasing depth makes you feel.

Related Books

Braun, Eric, and Sandra Donovan. *Bats.* Steck-Vaughn Company, 2002.

Clarke, Penny. *Spiders, Insects, and Minibeasts.* Franklin Watts, 2003.

Green, Tamara. *Scorpions.* Gareth Stevens Publishing, 1996.

Haffner, Marianne, and Hans-Peter B. Stutz. *Bats! Amazing and Mysterious Creatures of the Night.* Blackbirch Press, Inc., 1999.

Halfmann, Janet. *Scorpions: Nature's Predators.* Kidhaven Press, 2003.

Harman, Amanda. *Scorpions.* Grolier Educational, 2001.

Lassieur, Allison. *Scorpions: The Sneaky Stingers.* Franklin Watts, 2000.

Markle, Sandra. *Outside and Inside Bats.* Atheneum Books for Young Readers, 1997.

Pringle, Laurence. *Bats! Strange and Wonderful.* Boyds Mills Press, 2000.

— *Scorpion Man: Exploring the World of Scorpions.* Charles Scribner's Sons, 1994.

Richardson, Adele. *Scorpions.* Capstone Press, 2003.

Sherrow, Victoria. *Bats.* Lucent Books, Inc., 2001.

Taylor, Leighton. *Creeps From the Deep.* Chronicle Books, 1997.

Whitehouse, Patricia. *Bats.* Heinemann Library, 2003.

Interesting Web Sites

Bats: Learn more about these helpful creatures.

www.batcon.org/home/index.html
http://members.aol.com/obcbats/batinfo.html
www.eparks.org/wildlife_protection/wildlife_facts/bats/
www.worldalmanacforkids.com/explore/animals/bat.html
www.alienexplorer.com/ecology/topic21.html

Scorpions: Find out more information on these animals.

http://lsvl.la.asu.edu/askabiologist/research/scorpions/
www.szgdocent.org/ff/f-scorp.htm
www.desertusa.com/oct96/du_scorpion.html
www.museums.org.za/bio/scorpions/

Anglerfish: Explore pictures, information, and more about life in the deep sea.

http://web.ukonline.co.uk/aquarium/pages/anglerfish.html
http://ramseydoran.com/anglerfish/deep_sea.htm
www.pbs.org/wgbh/abyss/life/bestiary.html
www.mbayaq.org/efc/living_species/default.asp?hab=9
www.seasky.org/sea.html

Web sites have been carefully researched for accuracy, content, and appropriateness. However, teachers and caregivers are reminded that Web sites are subject to change. Internet use should always be monitored.

Strategies

BEFORE READING

Activate Prior Knowledge

by looking at the title, headings, pictures, and graphics to decide what I know about this topic.

DURING READING

Interact With Text

by identifying the main idea and supporting details.

AFTER READING

Evaluate

by searching the selection to determine how the author used evidence to reach conclusions.

LEARN
the *strategies*
in the selection
Maine Winters—Warm Ears
page 47

DANS CETTE MAISON
EST NÉ
LE 4 JANVIER 1809
Louis BRAILLE
INVENTEUR DE L'ECRITURE
EN POINTS SAILLANTS
POUR LES AVEUGLES

IL A OUVERT
A TOUS CEUX QUI NE VOIENT PAS
LES PORTES DU SAVOIR

IN THIS HOUSE
ON JANUARY 4 1809
WAS BORN
Louis BRAILLE
THE INVENTOR OF THE SYSTEM O...
WRITING IN RAISED DOTS FOR US...
BY THE BLIND

HE OPENED THE DOORS OF
KNOWLEDGE TO ALL THOSE
WHO CANNOT SEE

PRACTICE
the *strategies*
in the selection
Writing in the Dark
page 59

APPLY
the *strategies*
in the selection
Reading With Your Fingers
page 69

Think About the Strategies

BEFORE READING

Activate Prior Knowledge

by looking at the title, headings, pictures, and graphics to decide what I know about this topic.

My Thinking

The strategy says to look at the title, headings, pictures, and graphics to decide what I know about this topic.

The title is "Maine Winters—Warm Ears." The headings say something about being warmer, about setting up shop, and about remembering. Most of the pictures show people wearing something on their ears. And there's a drawing that looks like a plan for ear covers.

I know Maine is cold in the winter. I think this selection will be about how to keep ears warm in cold weather.

DURING READING

Interact With Text

by identifying the main idea and supporting details.

My Thinking

The strategy says to interact with the text by identifying the main idea and supporting details. I will stop and think about this strategy every time I come to a red button like this ⦿.

Maine Winters —Warm Ears

Keeping his ears warm was a real problem for Chester.

Chester Greenwood couldn't help it. His ears just couldn't stand the cold. And Maine winters are long and cold. This was a problem. The cold made Chester's tender ears turn chalk white. Then they turned beet red. Finally, they became dark blue.

It was 1873. Chester was 15 years old. And he was tired of going home early from sledding parties. He had tried keeping his ears warm. He wrapped a wool scarf around his head. However, the scarf would not stay in place. Also, the wool made his ears itch.

![Strategy]

Interact With Text by identifying the main idea and supporting details.

My Thinking

The main idea is about keeping warm in cold weather. I know this because the writer talks about ear covers and things that keep hands warm.

Then Chester had an idea. He thought of a way to cover his ears. At home, he bent two pieces of wire into loops. Each loop was big enough to circle around his ear. Then he attached the loops to the sides of a hat. His grandmother covered the loops with fur on the outside. And she put soft black velvet on the inside. She was sure that this would keep his ears warm.

Warmer Is Better

The first time Chester's friends saw his new invention, they laughed. But they were playing outside in the cold. Before long, they asked him to make ear covers for them, too.

Soon people all over Chester's hometown of Farmington, Maine, were asking for ear covers. His mother and grandmother helped him make more.

Chester called them Greenwood's Champion Ear Protectors. He began to sell them. His **customers** called them earmuffs. Maybe they took the name from hand muffs. Many women and girls used muffs in the winter back then. Muffs were warm tubes of wool or fur. Instead of wearing mittens or gloves, the ladies slipped a hand into each end of the tube to keep warm. Just as muffs kept hands warm, earmuffs kept ears warm.

Vo·cab·u·lar·y

customers (**kuhs**•tuh•muhrz) —people who buy things

Orders for Chester's earmuffs came in from all over New England. But he noticed that the fur-covered loops flopped around too much as the kids played. So Chester thought of a way to make his invention better.

He attached the loops to the ends of a metal strip. The strip fit over the person's head. There was a small bending piece called a **hinge**. It held the loop tight against the customer's head. When the person was finished wearing the earmuffs, they could be rolled up and stuffed into a pocket.

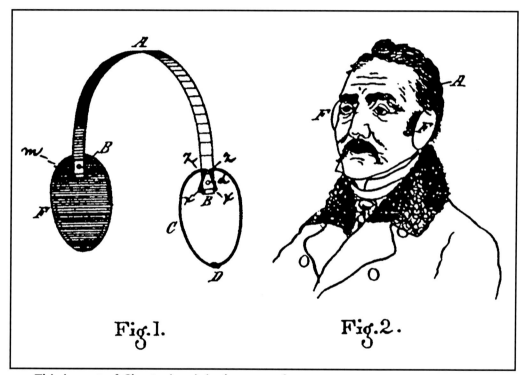

Fig.1.   Fig.2.

This is part of Chester's original request for a patent.

Setting Up Shop

In 1877, Chester received a **patent** from the United States Patent Office for his invention. That meant that no one else could make earmuffs. Chester set up a factory in his town. He called it The Shop. He designed special machines to make the earmuffs. Soon he was receiving many orders. He needed 20 full-time workers. By 1883, his factory was making 30,000 earmuffs a year. By 1936, the number had risen to 400,000!

Vo·cab·u·lar·y

hinge (hinj)—a kind of joint that allows something to bend back and forth

patent (pat•nt)—a right from the government that makes an inventor the only one who can make and sell the invention for a certain period of time

Strategy

Interact With Text by identifying the main idea and supporting details.

My Thinking

The main idea is that Chester's idea was a big success. The writer says that Chester got a patent for his earmuffs. He also set up a factory to make them. And he thought up new inventions, too.

Chester wasn't happy just to produce earmuffs, though. He went on to invent more than 130 other things. He received a patent for each one. One of his inventions is the whistling teakettle. It has a special kind of lip on its spout. As the water in the **kettle** begins to boil, it makes steam. The steam rises. It swirls upward into the spout. This steam strikes the bent lip of the spout. It makes a whistling sound.

Another of Chester's ideas was shock absorbers for cars. A shock absorber is a group of springs. They are attached to the wheels of the car. Car wheels hit a bump. The springs squeeze together. They soak up the bump. The riders barely feel a thing. Chester was also given a patent for his Florida Steam Heater. He invented a hook for pulling doughnuts out of boiling oil. He also made a rubberless rubber band and a steel rake.

Vo·cab·u·lar·y

kettle (ket·l)—a metal pot for boiling or cooking; often has a lid

Chester invented the Florida Steam Heater and a steel rake.

Farmington Remembers

Machines did most of the work in making Chester's earmuffs. But the machines back then had limits. They were not able to sew the warm fabric to the loops. Instead, the men and women of Farmington took the earmuffs home. They finished them there, by hand. At one time, half of the people in the county supported themselves and their families by finishing earmuffs. ⬤ . . . .

Strategy

Interact With Text by identifying the main idea and supporting details.

My Thinking
The main idea is that people had to finish the earmuffs by hand. Machines could not do all of the sewing. People in the town took them home to finish them. A lot of people ended up working for the earmuff factory.

Earmuffs are everywhere on Chester Greenwood Day!

Many people made money by working in Chester's factory. And the people of Farmington haven't forgotten Chester and his earmuffs. Every year, they celebrate Chester Greenwood Day. On that December day, everyone in town must wear earmuffs. Whoever is caught not wearing earmuffs must pay a fine! The money from the fines is helpful. It is used to support the local food bank.

The annual celebration begins with a parade. There are floats in the parade. Each must have something to do with earmuffs. At the end of the parade, the mayor introduces Chester and his wife Isabel. They present awards to the three best floats. But Chester died in 1937 at the age of 79. So actors happily play him and his wife. A highlight of the day is a quick dip in icy Clearwater Lake by members of the local Polar Bear Club. Speeches, workshops, and craft fairs complete the day.

Some visitors get a chance to meet Chester's great-grandson. His name is Ronald Greenwood. He still lives near Farmington. He says that most family members have a set or two of Chester's original ear protectors. They are more than 100 years old now.

What do you think Chester would say if he could see today's earmuffs? What might he think of the high-tech earmuffs designed to protect people from noise? What about earmuffs with built-in radios or attached CD players? Chances are, Chester would smile. He might say, "I wish I'd thought of that!"

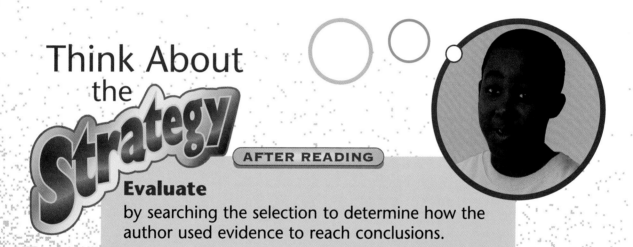

Think About
the
Strategy

AFTER READING

Evaluate
by searching the selection to determine how the author used evidence to reach conclusions.

My Thinking

The strategy says I should evaluate by searching the selection to see how the author used evidence to reach conclusions.

One conclusion is that earmuffs were a big success. At first, people laughed at Chester's invention. But soon a lot of people wanted to order earmuffs for themselves. Chester had to get a patent.

Then he opened up a factory to make earmuffs. A lot of people earned money working on earmuffs. Chester's invention made such a difference in the town that the people there have a celebration every year to remember him.

Graphic organizers help us organize information. I think this article can be organized by using a problem-solution frame. Here is how I organized the information.

Problem-Solution Frame
Maine Winters—Warm Ears

Problem Box

What is the problem?	Chester's ears were cold in the winter.
Why is it a problem?	He couldn't play outside very long.
Who has the problem?	Chester Greenwood

Solutions	Results
Chester made his first earmuffs with wire.	The muffs flapped too much.
He made a flexible metal band.	The muffs worked well.
Chester thought of many ways to improve products and to invent new things.	He invented more than 130 other things, including a whistling teakettle, car shock absorbers, and a steel rake.

Solution Box

End Result Box

Chester invented a useful product. He helped people in the town earn money, and he became famous. People in the town remember. Every year they celebrate Chester Greenwood Day.

I used my graphic organizer to write a summary of the article. Can you find the information in my summary that came from my problem-solution frame?

A Summary of
Maine Winters—Warm Ears

Chester Greenwood was 15, and he had a problem. His ears were freezing! He lived in Maine, where the winters are long and cold.

Chester wanted to play outside, so he solved his problem. He invented a way to keep his ears warm. He attached ear covers to his hat. At first, his friends laughed, but soon they wanted ear covers, too. They called them earmuffs.

Then Chester decided that his earmuffs flopped around too much. He thought of a way to make them better. He attached them to a metal strip. The strip fit over his head and kept the earmuffs in place.

Soon everyone wanted earmuffs. Chester set up a factory to make earmuffs for all his customers. Many people in his town had jobs in his factory. He became famous!

Chester kept thinking of ways to improve products, and he also went on to invent other useful things. He thought up how to make a teakettle that could signal when the water was hot. He made shock absorbers for cars, so riding would be smoother. And he invented a steel rake that wouldn't break so easily when big piles of leaves were being raked.

People in Farmington, Maine, still remember how Chester and his invention helped their town. Every year, they celebrate Chester Greenwood Day.

Introduction
Here is how I developed my introductory paragraph. I used information in the problem box in my problem-solution frame. It gives readers an idea of what they are about to read.

Body
I used information from the solutions and results boxes in my problem-solution frame in my body copy.

Conclusion
I summarized my paper by using the information in the end result box.

Compound Words

A **compound word** is a word formed from two smaller words. You can often figure out the meaning of the compound word by looking at the smaller words.

The word *earmuffs* appears in "Maine Winters—Warm Ears." *Earmuffs* is made of the words *ear* and *muffs*. The new word, *earmuffs,* means "the pads that fit over the ears." The pads keep the person's ears warm.

Other compound words in this story are:

grandmother = **grand** + **mother**, which means "the mother of one's father or mother"

teakettle = **tea** + **kettle**, which means "a special pot for boiling water, as for tea"

workshops = **work** + **shops**, which means "rooms or places where work is done"

Read the sentences below, and find the compound word in each one. Then, on a separate sheet of paper, write the compound words and the two smaller words that form each one. Predict what you think each compound word means, and write your predictions on the paper. Then check your predictions in a dictionary.

1. The scientist used the findings as a benchmark for judging future test results.

2. When others were in a panic, she was levelheaded and knew what to do.

3. If my brother and I start to argue, Mom steps in as the peacemaker.

4. We could tell how high the flood had been when we saw the watermark on the side of the building.

5. When Dad did all the chores in one day, Mom said he was a real workhorse.

Poetry

Here's an ad that might have appeared in a newspaper in Farmington, Maine, in early December. Practice this poem with a partner several times until you think you can perform it for an audience. Try alternating stanzas and reading the boldfaced line together.

> This poem is an advertisement that encourages people to come to the Farmington Fair. Read it as a radio announcer might. Use your voice to convince people to come to this exciting event.

Absolutely No Hats Allowed.

Bring your winter invention
to the Invention Convention
at the Farmington Fair.

You can bring lots of stuff
if you wear your earmuffs
at the Farmington Fair.

Absolutely No Hats Allowed.

Bring your toasty nose-heater
or a walk-around bird feeder
to the Farmington Fair.

Bring your weather rocker
or that chill-wind blocker
to the Farmington Fair.

Absolutely No Hats Allowed.

Invent a steamier kettle
and win a bright red medal
at the Farmington Fair.

Bring your winter display
and join the fun and the play
on Chester Greenwood Day!

Think About
the
Strategies

BEFORE READING

Activate Prior Knowledge
by looking at the title, headings, pictures, and graphics to decide what I know about this topic.

 Write notes on your own paper to tell how you used this strategy.

DURING READING

Interact With Text
by identifying the main idea and supporting details.

 When you come to a red button like this ⬤, write notes on your own paper to tell how you used this strategy.

Writing in the Dark

Becky Schroeder shared some of her findings at a school science fair.

Wouldn't it be great to write in the dark? Your brother or sister could turn off the light. They could go to sleep. But you could still finish your homework. It would be great at summer camp, too. You could write letters home after lights out. Doctors could take notes while they visited sleeping patients. Airplane pilots could take notes at night.

Becky Schroeder was only ten when she started inventing. She invented a way to write in the dark.

Becky was born in Toledo, Ohio, in 1962. One evening she was waiting in the car. Her mother was at a shopping center. Becky was trying to do her homework. But it was too dark for her to see. "If only I could write in the dark," she thought.

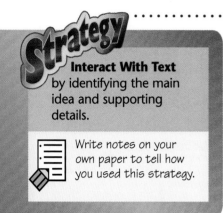
Becky finished her homework when she got home. But she kept thinking. She thought about ways to write in the dark. A week or so later, she went to the library. She wondered why some things glow.

Why Things Glow

Becky knew that some things glow because they're hot. But heat can be dangerous. How could you write if your paper was on fire? So Becky looked for things that glow without making a lot of heat.

Fireflies (lightning bugs) glow without becoming hot. Becky learned that this glow comes from inside the bugs. The bugs have something inside their bodies called **phosphorus**. Phosphorus comes into contact with a certain **protein** in their bodies. This causes light.

Becky learned the name for this light. The light comes from living things. Because of this, it is bioluminescence [by•oh•loo•muh•**nes**•uhns]. But Becky didn't think she could use bioluminescence to write in the dark.

She read some more. She found out that certain things absorb energy. Then they send some energy back into the air.

The energy that the materials soak up might be electricity. It could be rays from the sun. Or it could be X rays. The energy is sent back into the air. It takes the form of light. So after some materials absorb electricity, they glow.

Becky used electricity from small batteries in many of her early experiments.

Vo•cab•u•lar•y

phosphorus (fos•fuhr•uhs) —a certain chemical that is unstable and poisonous

protein (proh•teen)— a substance that living things need in order to work right

If the glow lasts only while the material is still absorbing energy, it's called **fluorescence**. Most class-rooms have fluorescent lights. They glow only while they receive electricity. The electricity stops. The glowing stops.

If the glow continues after the material is no longer receiving energy, it's called **phosphorescence**. Becky learned that some toys and watches have phosphorescent materials. That makes them glow in the dark.

Becky read about special paper stars that glow in the dark. Some people put them on the bedroom ceiling. The paper stars are phosphorescent. When the bedroom light is on, the stars absorb the light's energy. When the light is turned off, the stars keep glowing for a while.

Strategy

Interact With Text by identifying the main idea and supporting details.

Write notes on your own paper to tell how you used this strategy.

An Idea Becomes an Invention

Learning about phosphorescence gave Becky an idea. She would try something. She would cover a **clipboard** with phosphorescent paint. The paint would make the clipboard glow. Then she would put a sheet of paper on the glowing clipboard. Becky hoped her idea would work. In a dark room, the writing on the paper would show up. It would show as black letters against the glowing clipboard.

Becky's father helped her get some phosphorescent paint. Then she tried it out in the family bathroom. The bathroom had no windows. So it got really dark when the light was turned off. Becky tried several times. Then she yelled for her parents, "Come see! It works!"

Becky called her invention a Glo-Sheet. Her father was a lawyer. He helped her get a patent for it. Having a patent is important. No one else can copy or sell that product. The product belongs only to the inventor. Becky received a patent for her Glo-Sheet in August 1974. It came from the United States Patent and Trademark Office. At the time, she was 12 years old.

Her invention was a tablet of writing paper. It had a Glo-Sheet attached. The Glo-Sheet slipped under the top page. It made the page glow, except where there was writing. The writing stood out, black and clear!

Vo·cab·u·lar·y

fluorescence (flu•res•uhns)—the act of giving off light while being exposed to another source of energy

phosphorescence (fos•fuh•res•uhns)—the act of continuing to give off light after the removal of the energy source that caused the light to form

clipboard (klip•bord)—a small, flat board with a clip at the top for holding paper while writing

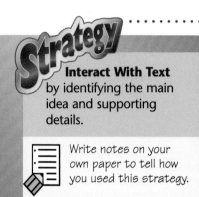
Becky Is Famous

Becky got her patent. Reporters from all around were excited. They rushed to tell everyone about it. She was named Ohio Inventor of the Year. She was **inducted** into the Ohio Inventors Hall of Fame.

By the time that first patent was official, though, Becky had thought of many ways to improve her Glo-Sheet.

Have you ever gone to a restaurant that was too dark? You could not read the menu? Becky thought of a way to make a menu glow. That way, you could read it in dim light. She also added lines to her Glo-Sheet to help people write neatly—in the dark!

Then Becky became concerned. Her Glo-Sheet stopped glowing after about 15 minutes. She figured out a way to help. She attached a battery to the Glo-Sheet. The writer pushes a button. The battery provides electrical energy. So the sheet glows for a longer time.

Becky kept thinking of ways to make her invention better. Each time, she applied for a new patent. She received almost a dozen patents in all.

Here, Becky is testing one of her Glo-Sheets in a dimly lit restaurant.

Vo·cab·u·lar·y

inducted (in·**dukt**·uhd)—admitted; invited to join

[62]

Over the next 20 years, Becky was asked to speak often. She was invited to many state and national meetings. She spoke about being an inventor. She also spoke at many schools and universities. Becky told young people not to be discouraged. Sometimes adults think they're too young to have a new idea.

Becky enjoyed sharing her story with young people. She hoped they would keep working on their ideas as she had done.

You Can Be an inventor, Too!

Have you ever thought about inventing something? As Becky said, "Childhood? That's when you start inventing!" But where do you begin? Well, there are many groups and organizations now that encourage young people to become inventors. They provide information for getting started. They also have competitions for young inventors.

The first thing is to have an idea. It could be an idea for something that has never been invented before. Or it could be an idea for improving something that has already

These young inventors entered an invention contest. Can you think of something you'd like to invent?

More Young Inventors

Name, grade	Invention	Description
Justin Riebeling, 6th grade	Speed Grain Cart	Wooden walls and a movable chute added to a kid's wagon help load, carry, and dispense grain.
Kayleigh C. Inkley, 5th grade	Parcel Pal	A padded, C-shaped hanger holds full plastic shopping bags, making it easier and less painful to carry them.
Jake S. Klimek, 5th grade	G.R.A.S.P.P. Device	This helps grasp, remove, and safely place a pan being taken from an oven.
Lisa M. Tripodi, 7th grade	Step-on Foot Opener	A ball placed over a doorknob and attached to a rod enables a foot to open a door.
Michael Allen Kitlas, 6th grade	Razor TT	Non-rusting wire and non-slip tape provide traction for a scooter on snow and ice.
Trey J. Wiler, 6th grade	Spyder Legs	Fold-down attachments to a ladder provide stability, especially on uneven surfaces.
Ashton C. Russell, 6th grade	Dirt Moist Fork	Water flowing down a tube on a pitchfork helps dampen and loosen soil for gardening.

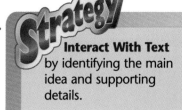

been invented. Decide what your invention is, what it will do, and how it will work. Write down your idea and all the thoughts you have about making the idea turn into a real invention.

Plan and make a model of your invention or a full-scale version of it. Test it every way you can. Keep records of the tests and all the outcomes. This record will help you make revisions and improvements. If you have any safety concerns, be sure to check with your parents or with another adult. When you are ready, you can submit your invention to an invention competition. Or you can apply for a patent on your own. Whichever choice you make, you will enjoy the experience of being a real inventor!

Strategy

Interact With Text by identifying the main idea and supporting details.

Write notes on your own paper to tell how you used this strategy.

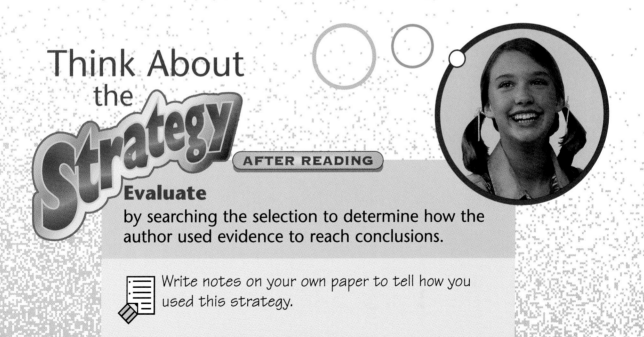

Think About the Strategy

AFTER READING

Evaluate

by searching the selection to determine how the author used evidence to reach conclusions.

Write notes on your own paper to tell how you used this strategy.

The Root *port*

Many English words and word parts come from other languages. *Port* is a root from the Latin word *portare,* meaning "to carry."

In "Writing in the Dark," we find this passage with a word that contains the root *port.*

> *Becky got her patent.* **Reporters** *from all around were excited.*

The word *reporters* is made of the root *port* and means "those who carry, or bring, the news."

Read the sentences below. Each contains a word with the root *port.* Think about the ways in which "to carry" is part of the meaning of each boldface word. On another sheet of paper, write the boldface words. Circle the root *port* in each one. Then, with a partner, discuss how "to carry" is a part of the meaning of each word. Use a dictionary if you need to.

1. The **porter** carried Bill's bags to his door.

2. We need to be at Gate 4 at the **airport** to catch our plane.

3. The artist took his **portfolio** to the meeting.

4. When we had to get our supplies overland from the river to the lake, we had to pay extra for **portage**.

5. The United States **imports** cars from other countries.

Poetry

Here is a poem that tells about Becky Schroeder's invention. Practice reading this poem until you can read it clearly and without hesitation.

> Read this poem several times until you almost have it memorized. As you practice, emphasize the first word in each line. Later, try emphasizing other words. Then decide which way of reading the poem sounds best.

Becky's Invention

Becky Schroeder stopped to wonder
how to write without a blunder.
Darkness makes a messy paper,
Becky said this is no caper.
Studied bugs that are phosphorous:
How things glow in the dark for us.
Light in a bug's own body sense
is by-oh-loo-muh-NES-uhns.

Learning about phosphorescence
helped her understand fluorescence.
To keep the glow a little longer,
clipboard 'n paper glow much stronger.
Watch the ink show up and glimmer.
With the paint, it won't grow dimmer.
Becky put the Glo-Sheet there
to brightly glow and even scare.

She worked the glow till it got finer.
Hunted glow light like a miner.
Now she's famous for asking "Why?"
Her Glo-Sheets are to buy!

Think About the  Strategies

BEFORE READING

Activate Prior Knowledge

by looking at the title, headings, pictures, and graphics to decide what I know about this topic.

DURING READING

Interact With Text

by identifying the main idea and supporting details.

AFTER READING

Evaluate

by searching the selection to determine how the author used evidence to reach conclusions.

 Use your own paper to jot notes to apply these Before, During, and After Reading Strategies. In this selection, you will choose when to stop, think, and respond.

READING WITH YOUR FINGERS

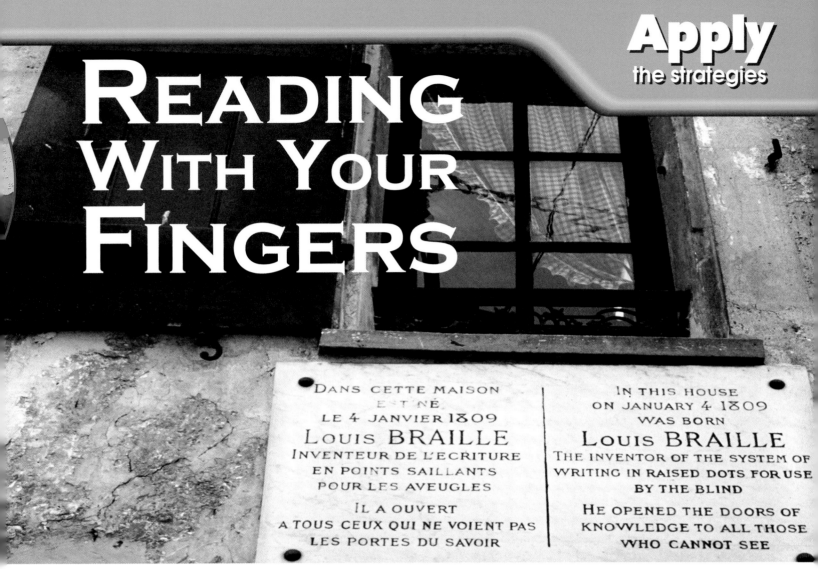

DANS CETTE MAISON
EST NÉ
LE 4 JANVIER 1809
LOUIS BRAILLE
INVENTEUR DE L'ÉCRITURE
EN POINTS SAILLANTS
POUR LES AVEUGLES

IL A OUVERT
A TOUS CEUX QUI NE VOIENT PAS
LES PORTES DU SAVOIR

IN THIS HOUSE
ON JANUARY 4 1809
WAS BORN
LOUIS BRAILLE
THE INVENTOR OF THE SYSTEM OF
WRITING IN RAISED DOTS FOR USE
BY THE BLIND

HE OPENED THE DOORS OF
KNOWLEDGE TO ALL THOSE
WHO CANNOT SEE

A plaque marks the house where Louis Braille was born.

Louis Braille [**loo**•ee brayl] was born in a small town in France in 1809. As a child, he loved to "help" his father make saddles and harnesses. One day when Louis was only three, he grabbed his father's **awl**. The boy tried to use the awl to punch a hole in some leather. But his little hand slipped. The awl made a hole in his left eye instead.

Vo • **cab** • u • lar • y

awl—a tool with a long, sharp point

If this had happened today, doctors probably could have saved Louis's eye. They would have gotten rid of the infection that was there. And they could have stopped that infection from making him blind in his right eye, too. But in 1812, no one knew how to cure infections. Within two years, Louis was blind in both eyes.

Also, if this had happened today, Louis could have attended special schools. He could have learned as much as any other child attending school. But back then, blind people were not taught to read or write. Many ended up begging on the streets.

Louis's family took good care of him, though. They helped him learn to get around his house. Then they helped him in the village. In time, Louis learned to recognize 600 villagers. He could tell by the sound of their footsteps! He could identify birds by their songs. He knew flowers by their smell.

His oldest sister, Catherine, helped him learn to read a few words. She made letters out of straw so he could feel their shapes. Louis did so well that he was accepted at the local school when he was only seven years old. He listened carefully. He memorized what the teacher said. Louis could figure out the answers to math problems before any of his classmates. Yet he was sad. He could not read the school's books.

With his sister's help, Louis learned to use his fingers to feel the shape of alphabet letters.

Louis Goes Away to School

About the time Louis turned ten, his parents decided to send him to the National Institute for the Young Blind, in Paris. This special school was four hours from his home. His parents did not want to send him away. But Louis needed to learn as much as possible. He had to be able to support himself when he was older. The institute would help him.

At first, Louis was lonely and frightened at his new school. The other blind boys played tricks on him. They stole his food. They locked him in the bathroom. After a while, though, they became his friends.

Louis learned quickly. He was very excited when he was allowed to read the 14 special books at the school library. These books were printed with raised letters. The letters had to be big enough to be felt. So not many words would fit on a page. This made the books very big. In fact, each book had to be divided into 20 volumes. This made them like an encyclopedia. Each volume weighed 20 pounds! These books were not easy to read either. It was hard to feel the difference between such letters as **m** and **n**.

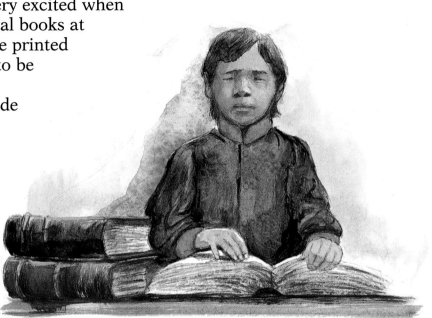

Louis was learning to "read" with his fingers.

Louis Starts Experimenting

Louis knew there had to be a way to make books so blind people could read them. He began to try out different things. Once, he tried punching little holes in paper. The holes formed a **code**. But this code was hard to learn. And it was hard to read just using fingers.

The teachers at the institute knew Louis was searching for a new way to make books. They did not expect him to succeed. After all, he was just a boy—and he was blind!

When Louis was 12, a man named Captain Charles Barbier [bar•bee•yay] spoke to the students at the institute. This man had invented a code of raised dots and dashes. Each pattern stood for a different sound. Barbier called it "night writing." He had invented it so soldiers on a battlefield could read messages without using a light.

At last, Louis knew how he would make his new books. He would use a tool called a **stylus**. It would make raised dots and dashes on paper. For 3 years, Louis worked on his new system of writing. Often he worked at night. The other boys at the institute were asleep.

Louis was only 15 in 1824. He finally showed his new idea to his classmates. They loved it! They named it after him. They called it the Braille method.

Vo•cab•u•lar•y

code (kohd)—a kind of secret writing

stylus (sty•luhs)—a tool for pressing marks into clay, paper, etc.

A	B	C	D	E	F	G	H	I	J
1	2	3	4	5	6	7	8	9	10

K	L	M	N	O	P	Q	R	S	T

U	V	W	X	Y	Z

This chart shows how the large and small dots are arranged to stand for each letter of the alphabet.

Louis's Invention Goes Unnoticed

Louis kept on improving his idea. He stopped using dashes. Instead he used from one to six dots to stand for each letter. Each letter had a different number and placement of dots.

In 1826, Louis graduated from the institute. Then he became a teacher there—at the age of 17! He also played the organ at a church near the school. Louis used the money he earned and all his extra time to copy books into Braille. He had someone read books aloud so he could create the words with patterns of dots.

Strangely, the other teachers at the institute did not help him. They were **jealous** of what he had done. Students were punished if they were caught using Braille. In 1843, the principal burned some of the books Louis had so carefully created. However, Louis and some of the boys at the school did not give up. Finally, in 1844, the principal allowed the use of Braille. That was 20 years after Louis had invented it.

The rest of the world, too, was slow to use this new method. Louis died of **tuberculosis** in 1852. He was only 43. People knew him more as a church organist than as

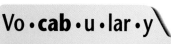

Louis loved to play the organ, but reading and writing music were hard to do.

Vo·cab·u·lar·y

jealous (**jel**•uhs)—full of envy or suspicion

tuberculosis (tu•bur•kyuh•**loh**•sis)—a disease of the lungs

the inventor of Braille. And it was 1917 before the United States government approved Braille.

Now, people all over the world use Braille. They send Braille greeting cards. They use Braille computers. And they read directions on elevators in Braille. Louis Braille, a blind boy who just wanted to be able to read, has helped millions of other people do so.

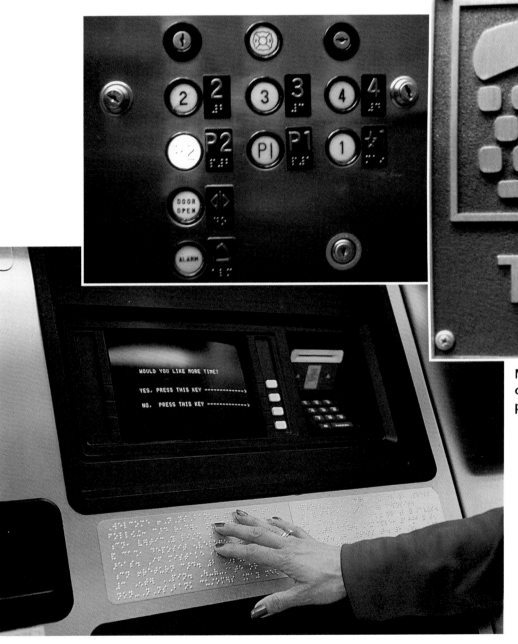

Many modern inventions can be adapted for use by people who cannot see.

Vocabulary

Context Clues

To figure out an unknown word, use **context clues** to help you. Look at the words near the unknown word. Look at the sentences nearby. They will give you clues to the word's meaning.

Read this passage from "Reading With Your Fingers."

> *One day when Louis was only three, he grabbed his father's **awl**. The boy tried to use the **awl** to punch a hole in some leather.*

You can use context clues to figure out the meaning of *awl*. The word *grabbed* is a context clue. It tells you that an awl can be held. Now look at the phrase *punch a hole*. It suggests that an *awl* is a tool that someone uses to punch holes in leather.

Use context clues as you read these passages from "Reading With Your Fingers." They will help you understand the meanings of *infection* and *institute*.

> *If this had happened today, doctors probably could have saved Louis's eye. They would have gotten rid of the **infection** that was there.*

> *About the time Louis turned ten, his parents decided to send him to the National **Institute** for the Young Blind, in Paris. This special school was four hours from his home.*

Now, on another sheet of paper, write definitions for *infection* and *institute*. Tell what context clues helped you understand the meanings of these words. Use a dictionary to check your definitions.

Letter

Louis Braille probably found ways to write letters home while he was away at school. He might have asked a teacher to write a letter something like this for him on this very important day in his life. Of course, the letter would have been written in French. Here's an English version of what Louis might have written to his family. Practice reading this letter until you can read it with good expression and appropriate phrasing.

Fluency TIP

As you practice reading this letter aloud, imagine yourself as Louis Braille writing to his family. Try to make your voice show the feelings that he must have felt as he told about his loneliness at his school and later the excitement he felt as he described his new writing system.

14 March 1824

Dear Mother, Father, and Catherine,

Remember when you first brought me to this school? I wanted to come here so I could learn. But I didn't realize how lonely I would be. I still miss all of you an awful lot! But now I have a surprise to tell you about.

Today I knew that my friends are really my friends! For today I uncovered my new idea. Let me tell you about it.

You know how important it is to me that blind people be able to read all the things you do. Well, ever since Captain Charles Barbier was here, I have been working with this man's code of raised dots and dashes. Captain Barbier made up patterns for different sounds. He called it "night writing."

Captain Barbier gave me the push I needed. I've been working every day with his code and with my stylus to make a book. Well, I showed it to everyone. And guess what? My friends were so excited about it, they named my method after me! Just think! Soon everyone will be using the Braille method.

No more carrying around 20-pound books! What do you think of that? Come visit soon and see the new Braille method.

Your happy son,
Louis

Application Form

Applying for Membership

A group of young inventors meets every week. Here is the application form for joining the club. Look at the form, and then answer the questions on the next page.

APPLICATION FORM—YOUNG INVENTORS' CLUB
Meetings: Monday, 7:00 PM, at the Weston Town Library
(except holidays)
Contact Person: Tim Woodson, Librarian

Name _____ Age _____

Address _____

_____

Phone Number _____

E-mail Address _____

School _____ Grade _____

Special Interests _____

Inventions _____

_____

Parent's or Guardian's Signature _____

Date _____

Discussion Questions

Answer these questions with a partner or on a separate sheet of paper.

1. Let's say you like to invent things that work with batteries. Where would you write that on the application form?

2. Which of these Mondays is not a meeting day for the club?
   a. June 27
   b. July 4
   c. July 11
   d. July 18

3. A "contact person" is listed on the form. When should you try to reach this person?
   a. when you have an idea for an invention
   b. when you want to know the club's meeting time
   c. when you want to know the club's meeting place
   d. when you want to join the club

4. The application form asks for your school and grade. What does this probably mean?
   a. Only students from certain schools are allowed to join the club.
   b. Only students in certain grades are allowed to join the club.
   c. Mr. Woodson wants to know where club members go to school.
   d. Mr. Woodson likes some schools better than others.

5. Which action should you do first?
   a. Fill out this form.
   b. Meet with Mr. Woodson to find out more about the club.
   c. Ask your parent or guardian to sign the form.
   d. Go to a club meeting.

6. Why does the form ask for the signature of a parent or guardian?

7. Why do you think this club has an application form?

8. Evaluate this application form. What would you add or leave out? Explain your answer.

Tell About an Inventor

Choose an inventor or an invention. Gather information about that choice, and make a report or a display.

Glow-in-the-Dark Experiment

Collect several glow-in-the-dark items. Experiment to see how the length of time each is exposed to light compares with how long it glows. Make a chart or table to display your findings.

Write in Braille

Find a copy of the Braille alphabet. Press the blunt end of an object such as a ball point pen into the back of a piece of medium-weight paper to make a pattern of raised dots that conveys a series of words or a message.

Be an Inventor

Think of something that you would like to invent. Write a description of what the invention is, how you would go about making one, and what it would do. You might want to include drawings or illustrations.

Write a Play

Imagine that the real Chester Greenwood was able to attend a modern Chester Greenwood Day celebration. Develop a short play in which you and your friends can be the actors. The roles could be Chester, his wife, his great-grandson, and town leaders. Make sure Chester understands, in the play, what his inventions have meant to Farmington.

"Meet" an Inventor

Which inventor, past or present, would you like to meet and talk with? Imagine that this meeting has taken place. Write a journal entry or a magazine article that describes the meeting. Tell the main ideas the two of you discussed. Be sure to include supporting details.

Related Books

Blashfield, Jean F. *Women Inventors.* Capstone Press, Inc., 1996.

Brill, Marlene Targ. *Margaret Knight: Girl Inventor.* The Millbrook Press, 2001.

Casey, Susan. *Women Invent: Two Centuries of Discoveries That Have Shaped Our World.* Chicago Review Press, 1997.

Currie, Stephen. *Women Inventors.* Lucent Books, 2001.

Fradin, Dennis. *Louis Braille: The Blind Boy Who Wanted to Read.* Silver Press, 1997.

Freedman, Dennis. *Out Of Darkness: The Story of Louis Braille.* Clarion Books, 1997.

Hegedus, Alannah, and Kaitlin Rainey. *Shooting Hoops and Skating Loops: Great Inventions in Sports.* Tundra Books, 1999.

McClure, Judy. *Theoreticians and Builders: Mathematicians, Physical Scientists, Inventors.* Raintree Steck-Vaughn Publishers, 2000.

Pasternak, Ceel, and Linda Thornburg. *Cool Careers for Girls in Computers.* Impact Publications, 1999.

St. George, Judith. *So You Want to Be an Inventor?* Philomel Books, 2002.

Thimmesh, Catherine. *Girls Think of Everything: Stories of Ingenious Inventions by Women.* Houghton Mifflin Company, 2002.

Tucker, Tom. *Brainstorm! The Stories of Twenty American Kid Inventors.* Farrar, Straus & Giroux, 1995.

Williams, Brian. *Science.* Heinemann Library, 2002.

Woog, Adam. *Bill Gates.* KidHaven Press, 2003.

Interesting Web Sites

Choose any of these sites to learn more about inventors, inventing, and inventions.

www.inventionatplay.org/
www.si.edu/lemelson/centerpieces/ilives/
www.invent.org/hall_of_fame/1_0_0_hall_of_fame.esp
www.invent.org/book/index.html
www.si.edu/resource/faq/nmah/invent.htm
www.colitz.com/site/wacky.htm
www.nsta.org/programs/craftsman
www.enchantedlearning.com/inventors/
www.pbs.org/wgbh/amex/telephone/sfeature/

BEFORE READING

Set a Purpose
by using the title and headings to write questions that I can answer while I am reading.

DURING READING

Clarify Understanding
by using photographs, charts, and other graphics to help me understand what I'm reading.

AFTER READING

Respond
by drawing logical conclusions about the topic.

LEARN
the strategies
in the selection
And the Winds Blew
page 83

PRACTICE
the **strategies**
in the selection
And the Earth Shakes
page 95

APPLY
the strategies
in the selection
And the Earth Explodes
page 105

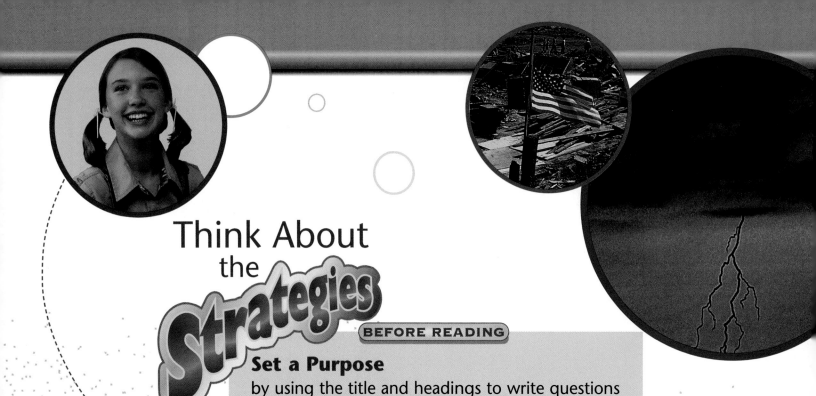

Think About
the
Strategies

Set a Purpose

by using the title and headings to write questions that I can answer while I am reading.

My Thinking

The strategy says to set a purpose by using the title and headings to write questions I can answer while I am reading. The title is "And the Winds Blew." My question is "What winds blew and where did they blow?" The first heading is "Another Monster Tornado." My question is "What is a monster tornado?"

The next headings are "Closet Saves Lives," "City in Tatters," and "Picking Up the Pieces." These make me want to know what happened. The last heading is "Helping the Homeless." I want to know who was homeless and how they lost their homes. Now I'm ready to read and find answers to my questions.

DURING READING

Clarify Understanding

by using photographs, charts, and other graphics to help me understand what I'm reading.

My Thinking

The strategy says to clarify understanding by using photographs, charts, and other graphics to help me understand what I'm reading. I will stop and think about this strategy every time I come to a red button like this ⬤.

[82]

And the Winds Blew

The day started out to be nice in Vernon, Texas. Not long after lunch, though, black clouds started to roll in. Then the thunder and lightning started. **Gusts** of wind shook shutters. They bent trees almost to the ground. It was a bad storm.

At 3:30 in the afternoon, it got worse. **Tornado** sirens sounded. People knew what that meant. Tornadoes were forming nearby. Most of the people there took shelter. They went into **storm cellars**. They rushed to basements, closets, or bathrooms. It was good that they did. Just a few minutes earlier, a huge tornado touched down. It was just outside Vernon.

Vo•cab•u•lar•y

gusts (guhsts)—short, sudden bursts of wind

tornado (tor•**nay**•doh)— violent spinning winds, also called funnel cloud

storm cellars (**storm sel**•uhrz)—underground shelters in or near a house, for protection from bad storms

Strategy

Clarify Understanding by using photographs, charts, and other graphics to help me understand what I'm reading.

My Thinking
The photograph at the beginning of this story helps me understand what the people in the story must be going through. That looks like a very bad storm!

The sky had turned black. The **funnel cloud** was huge. Eleven-year-old Jonetta Thomas was just getting home from school. "I couldn't see my hand in front of my face. It was so dark," she said. "I heard a roaring sound. It was like a train coming right at me."

Jonetta barely made it into the storm cellar. The tornado passed right over Jonetta's house. It destroyed it. Still, Jonetta herself was lucky. She wasn't hurt.

A teacher from a grade school in Vernon was just as lucky. She was rushing home after school. She was trying to beat the storm. Suddenly, the tornado swept up her car. The high winds spun her car around in the air. Then it dropped the teacher and her car to the ground. The teacher **survived**.

Other people in Vernon did not escape harm. Many died. Dozens of people were hurt. Many homes and businesses were damaged. Or, like Jonetta's house, they were blown to pieces. But some people, like the teacher, survived. And they had been very scared.

Another Monster Tornado

It was fifty miles away and two and a half hours later. People in Wichita Falls, Texas, were getting dinner on the table. Just then, the sirens sounded. It was just past 6:00 PM. The following news came on the TV and radio.

Vo·cab·u·lar·y

funnel cloud (fun•uhl klowd)—a cloud shaped like a long tube, moving quickly and sometimes touching the ground, also called a tornado

survived (sur•vyvd)— stayed alive

TORNADO WARNING

Wichita Falls, Texas • The National Weather Service has issued a tornado warning. It is in effect until 7 PM CST (Central Standard Time) for Wichita County of Texas and the city of Wichita Falls, Texas. At 5:58 PM CST radar showed a tornado ten miles southwest of town. At 6:00 PM CST a spotter saw a tornado. It was 5 miles southwest of the Wichita Falls Memorial Stadium. It is moving northeast at 30 miles an hour. Persons in Wichita Falls should take cover right away.

Then the televisions and radios of Wichita Falls were quiet. The houses went dark. The power was out. Most people in the town saw the warnings. They heard the sirens and rushed to take cover. Then a tornado roared by.

Most tornadoes are narrow. They cause damage in a narrow path. This tornado was even larger than the tornado that struck Vernon. It was ½ mile across. Its winds reached 300 miles per hour! **Meteorologists** think that 3 separate funnels joined to make this giant tornado.

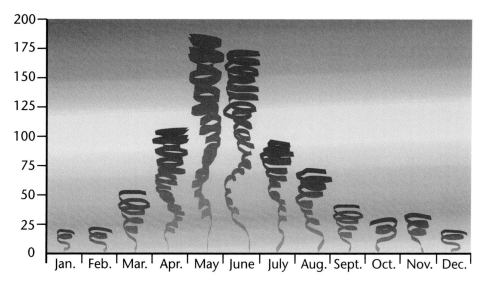

This bar graph shows the average number of tornadoes in the United States each month during the years 1950–2000.

Closet Saves Lives

"I never thought I'd want to thank a closet." That's what one Wichita Falls resident said after the tornado. Only the closet of that person's home was left standing. Three people had hidden there. They could hear the roar of the tornado. They could hear the sounds of their house blowing apart. They could feel it when the roof was pulled off the house.

"I've never been so scared," the resident added. "We just stayed together in the closet until it got quiet outside."

The tornado that hit Wichita Falls smashed glass. It sent pieces flying through the air. It blew buildings away as if they were made of toothpicks. It sucked cars up into

Vo•cab•u•lar•y

meteorologists (mee•tee•uh•**rol**•uh•jists)— scientists who study and try to predict the weather

the air. It carried them hundreds of feet before dropping them. Pieces of houses and furniture were found a mile away from where they belonged.

Tornado damage in Texas

City in Tatters

The tornado left Wichita Falls in a mess. The town looked as if it had been bombed. The **debris** of destroyed buildings, smashed cars, and broken furniture was everywhere. It was spread out across a path 10 miles long. Pictures, clothing, and dishes were scattered all over.

Many people lost their lives. Hundreds of people were hurt. Thousands of people (20,000, to be exact) were left homeless. This meant that 1 out of every 5 people who lived there was left without a home.

There were many stories to tell. But some stories stood out. For example, the National Guard of Wichita Falls had gathered at their **armory**. They were getting ready to go to Vernon. They were going to help clean up tornado damage in that town.

Then they heard a sound like a freight train. The sound roared over their heads. The 60 officers hurried to take shelter. Their armory was destroyed. But they survived.

Vo·cab·u·lar·y

debris (duh•bree)—
smashed and broken pieces of walls, wood, bricks; ruins

armory (ar•muh•ree)—
a place for training military reserves

They didn't need to travel 50 miles away to help clean up storm damage. They had enough to clean up right where they were!

At a restaurant in downtown Wichita Falls, a **frantic** manager told the customers to stop eating. He said to follow him to the back of the restaurant. Seconds later, the tornado tore off the roof. Then it tossed it back down on the building. The walls were crushed. Three people were killed. But many more would have died if the manager had not acted so quickly.

Tornado damage in Saratoga, Texas

April 10, 1979, is one of the worst days in the history of tornadoes. In Oklahoma and Texas, 10 tornadoes killed 62 people on that day. ◉

Picking Up the Pieces

Nothing could make up for the lives lost in the tornadoes in April 1979. But compared with how much damage was done, the number of deaths was low. Television and radio reports did just what they were supposed to do. So did the warning sirens. They warned people ahead of time to take **shelter**. Without the warnings, even more people might have died.

Next came the cleanup. People started picking up the pieces. They had to start putting together their homes and

Strategy

Clarify Understanding by using photographs, charts, and other graphics to help me understand what I'm reading.

My Thinking
I have heard that "a picture is worth a thousand words." This photograph really helps me understand how terrible the damage from a tornado can be.

Vo·**cab**·u·lar·y

frantic (**fran**•tik)—very nervous, scared

shelter (**shel**•tur)—something that gives protection

[87]

their lives. Volunteers helped dig people out of damaged buildings. People at hospitals worked around the clock to save lives. They treated those who were hurt.

The electric companies called in extra people. They had to get power back on.

Neighbors helped each other sort through all the mess. They tried to find anything they could save from their homes. Homemade signs appeared in places where buildings had once stood. "Gone with the Wind," one said. "We're off to see the Wizard," said another. People were cleaning up by joking with each other. And they had great support for one another.

Helping the Homeless

Soon the tornadoes were past. Right away, calls were put out for help. There are groups that help people in need. Two of these, the Salvation Army and the Red Cross, went to the towns. They set up **emergency** centers. They gave food, clothing, and shelter to those who needed it. Mobile homes were brought in to give people places to live.

This sign shows places people could go for help after a disaster in that area.

Vo•**cab**•u•lar•y

emergency
(i•**mur**•juhn•see)—set up for a disaster

These towns were destroyed in just a few minutes. But it has taken many years to rebuild them. In some cases just a **foundation** was left. This was all there was to remind people that a family once lived there. Those who lived through the tornadoes will remember. They will talk about that "Terrible Tuesday."

Think About the Strategy

AFTER READING

Respond
by drawing logical conclusions about the topic.

My Thinking
The strategy says that I should respond by drawing logical conclusions about the topic. Well, I know now that tornadoes are terrible storms that do a lot of damage and can hurt or kill people. I understand how important it is to listen to storm warnings on TV, on the radio, or when my town's warning siren goes off.

After reading the selection, I know to take shelter in a storm cellar or in a closet or bathroom. People in the story stayed safe when they did that. I think remembering these logical conclusions might save my life someday.

Organizing Information

A web helps us organize information about one main topic. The web shows relationships of details to the main topic and to other details. The main topic goes in the center circle. Related details go in smaller circles connected to the center circle.

Web

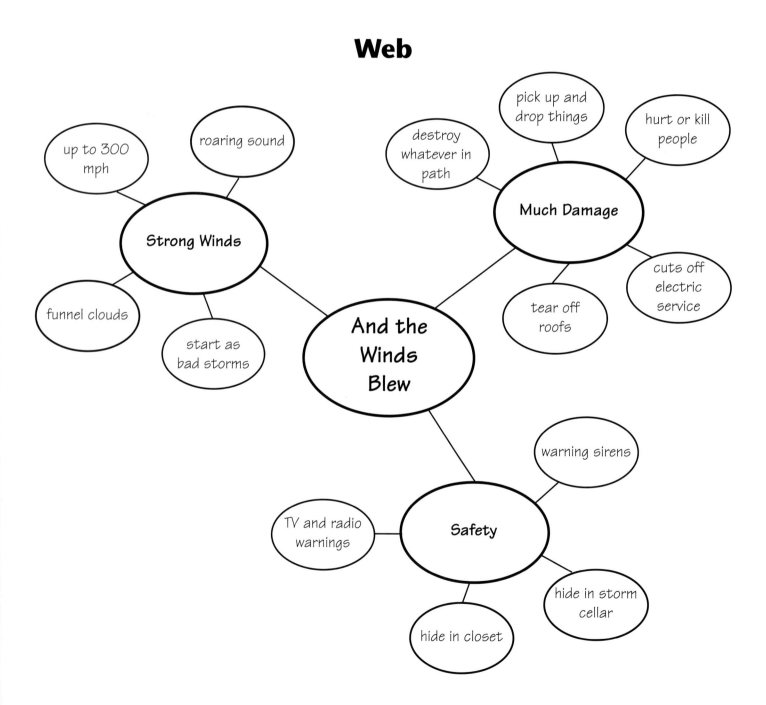

- up to 300 mph
- roaring sound
- **Strong Winds**
- funnel clouds
- start as bad storms
- **And the Winds Blew**
- destroy whatever in path
- pick up and drop things
- hurt or kill people
- **Much Damage**
- tear off roofs
- cuts off electric service
- warning sirens
- TV and radio warnings
- **Safety**
- hide in closet
- hide in storm cellar

I used my graphic organizer to write a summary of the article. Can you find the information in my summary that came from my web?

A Summary of
And the Winds Blew

Tornadoes are powerful. They can do a lot of damage. Still, if you know what to do, you can stay safe.

A tornado starts as a bad storm. If you hear a roaring sound during a bad storm, a tornado might be coming. A tornado is a very strong wind that moves in a circle. The wind forms a funnel cloud. This wind can blow up to 300 miles per hour.

A tornado can destroy anything in its path. It can pick up a car and carry it hundreds of feet. A tornado can tear the roof off a building—and then blow the walls away. Even if your house is not damaged, you may not have power for many days. Tornadoes often blow down power lines.

To stay safe during a bad storm, listen for television and radio warnings. Your town may have tornado sirens. If you hear them, take shelter. Go to a safe place, such as a storm cellar or a basement. If you do not have a basement, hide in a closet.

Stay calm! A tornado does not last long. When it is gone, you can help your neighbors with the cleanup.

Introduction
Here is my introduction. It tells what I will write about. The main idea is in the center of my web.

Body
The first paragraph of my body copy has details from the web bubble "Strong Winds." The next two paragraphs are based on the other two bubbles and the ideas connected to each of them.

Conclusion
I summarized my paper by recalling the main ideas.

Onomatopoeia

Some words come from sounds. For example, the word *buzz* comes from the sound an insect's wings make when it is flying. **Onomatopoeia** [on•uh•mat•uh•pee•uh] is the use of words such as "buzz" and "slurp" that come from sounds.

Onomatopoeia is often used to make descriptive writing and poetry more interesting. The article "And the Winds Blew" is very descriptive. The writer wants you to know what being in a tornado might be like. Read the following sentence from the story:

> *The tornado that hit Wichita Falls **smashed** glass.*

The word *smash* comes from the sound made when something is broken into many pieces. Smash means "to hit, drop, or run into something causing it to break into many pieces." The meaning of the word is closely related to the pronunciation and sound of the word.

Read the list of words softly to yourself. The first three words are used in "And the Winds Blew." Think about what each word's sound tells you about its meaning. Then, on a separate sheet of paper, write a sentence about when or how you might hear each word. For example, you might write, "I hear a zap when a mosquito hits the bug zapper on a summer night."

1. roar
2. rush
3. gust
4. clatter
5. squish

6. screech
7. sputter
8. hiss
9. zap
10. growl

Book Excerpt

Before Dorothy lands in Oz, in the book *The Wonderful Wizard of Oz,* she has a terrifying experience. As a tornado tears through Kansas, Dorothy and her family scramble for shelter. As you read this passage, think about the selection "And the Winds Blew."

Fluency TIP

Read the passage in a way that your voice expresses the danger of the coming tornado. Continue to practice until your voice shows the fear and danger the writer meant to express.

From **The Wonderful Wizard of Oz**
by L. Frank Baum

Suddenly Uncle Henry stood up.

"There's a cyclone coming, Em," he called to his wife. "I'll go look after the stock." Then he ran toward the sheds where the cows and horses were kept.

Aunt Em dropped her work and came to the door. One glance told her of the danger close at hand.

"Quick, Dorothy!" she screamed. "Run for the cellar!"

Toto jumped out of Dorothy's arms and hid under the bed, and the girl started to get him. Aunt Em, badly frightened, threw open the trap door in the floor and climbed down the ladder into the small, dark hole. Dorothy caught Toto at last and started to follow her aunt. When she was halfway across the room there came a great shriek from the wind, and the house shook so hard that she lost her footing and sat down suddenly upon the floor.

Then a strange thing happened.

The house whirled around two or three times and rose slowly through the air. Dorothy felt as if she were going up in a balloon.

The north and south winds met where the house stood, and made it the exact center of the cyclone. In the middle of a cyclone the air is generally still, but the great pressure of the wind on every side of the house raised it up higher and higher, until it was at the very top of the cyclone; and there it remained and was carried miles and miles away as easily as you could carry a feather.

Think About
the
Strategies

Set a Purpose

by using the title and headings to write questions that I can answer while I am reading.

 Write notes on your own paper to tell how you used this strategy.

DURING READING

Clarify Understanding

by using photographs, charts, and other graphics to help me understand what I'm reading.

 When you come to a red button like this ⦿, write notes on your own paper to tell how you used this strategy.

And the Earth Shakes

It was 1994. The ground beneath Northridge, California, shook with a huge force. It was an **earthquake**. It was one of the worst in the United States. Fifty-seven people died. Hundreds were hurt. Thousands of homes were destroyed. Roads and freeways were closed.

There are millions of earthquakes a year. Most are small. They are not felt. But **sensitive** scientific equipment alerts us. Hundreds of quakes are strong enough to be felt. They can even change the shape of Earth.

There was an earthquake in Kobe [**koh**•bay], Japan. It hit one year after the Northridge quake. It was twice as strong. It killed 5,500 people. And 30,000 were left home-less. The quake destroyed nearly 200,000 buildings. But the ground shook for less than a minute.

Sometimes movements in the earth can be seen on the surface.

Vo•cab•u•lar•y

earthquake (**urth**•kwayk)— a sudden movement in part of the earth's crust

sensitive (**sen**•si•tiv)— able to sense very small changes or very small quakes in the earth

[95]

The Why and How of an Earthquake

A layer of rocks covers Earth. This layer is 5 to 35 miles deep. It is called the earth's **crust**. This crust is very thin compared with the size of the earth. Earthquakes take place in the crust. Cracks run through the rocks in the crust, just like a crack in a sidewalk. The cracks are called faults.

The crust floats on a layer of Earth that is 1,800 miles thick. That layer is called the **mantle**. It is made of heavy, melted rock. This melted rock moves under the crust. It has broken the crust up into big, flat sections. These sections are called **plates**.

The plates are always moving. They may move as much as 4 inches a year. Sometimes they bump against each other. Sometimes they pull away from each other. Two plates may grind against each other. This may cause an earthquake.

The rocks on each side of the fault push against each other. This makes energy build up. **Friction** holds the rocks in place for a long time. But the energy builds up. After a while, it becomes stronger than the friction. The rocks move along the fault. The spot where the movement takes place is called the earthquake focus.

In a small earthquake, the grinding may last for a second or two. A large earthquake is different. It may last for several minutes. **Aftershocks** are weaker than the first shock. They may follow a quake for several weeks. The rocks along the fault are settling into their new positions.

The Where of an Earthquake

There is an area called the Ring of Fire. It circles the Pacific Ocean. Four out of every five earthquakes happen along this ring. Places that border on the Ring of Fire include parts of New Zealand, Japan, and China. It also has the west coasts of the United States, Mexico, Colombia, Peru, and Chile, and the countries of Central America.

Most earthquakes happen around the Ring of Fire. But they can occur anywhere. For instance, a quake zone runs across southern Europe through the Middle East and into Asia.

Vo·cab·u·lar·y

crust (krust)—Earth's outer-most layer of solid rock

mantle (**man**•tl)—the layer of Earth between the crust and the core, or center

plates (playts)—the sections of Earth's crust that float above the mantle

friction (**frik**•shuhn)—the rubbing of one thing against another

aftershocks (**af**•tuhr•shoks)—smaller quakes after the main earthquake in a certain area

[96]

The Ring of Fire

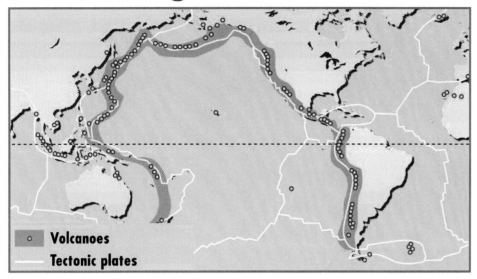

○ **Volcanoes**

— **Tectonic plates**

In the United States, most earthquakes take place in California. In fact, almost half of all our earthquakes occur there. There are only a few places in the United States where no quakes have ever been recorded. These places are in parts of Texas, Alabama, and Florida. That doesn't mean earthquakes have never happened there. They just haven't happened since people started keeping records of them.

Measuring and Comparing Earthquakes

Some earthquakes cause a lot of harm to people. They can damage or destroy buildings. Other earthquakes are barely felt. Can you tell how big an earthquake is by how much damage it does? The answer is no.

Earthquakes that cause a lot of damage may be big. But they also cause damage because they are close to where people live. Even a medium-sized quake close to a big city can be a problem. It may destroy buildings and hurt people. But a very large quake in a place like a desert may not be bad. It will not damage buildings or hurt people. This is because no one lives there.

Scientists have found a way to measure earthquakes. They measure how hard the shaking is. They do this with a **seismograph**. A seismograph can measure even tiny earthquake **tremors** many miles away. It contains a roll of paper. The paper turns on a drum. A pen traces a line onto the paper.

Vo·cab·u·lar·y

seismograph (**syz**•muh•graf)—a scientific instrument that senses and records movements in or on the ground, especially earthquakes

tremors (**trem**•urz)— quivering movements before or after an earthquake

Geologists measure earthquake damage in California.

When a quake occurs, the line on the paper goes up and down very fast. This makes a jagged line. A large quake makes a more jagged line than a small quake.

Scientists have set up seismographs at many places on Earth. They compare all the records. This helps them find out when the shocks from one quake arrived at different places. In this way, they can learn exactly where the earthquake's focus is underground. They can also find the earthquake's strength and its **epicenter**. The epicenter is the place where the quake started.

Have you heard earthquakes rated by numbers? Sometimes people on the news will talk about a "magnitude-5" earthquake. They are using numbers from the Richter [**rik**•tur] scale. It goes from 1–10. The Richter scale measures the strength of an earthquake. Each number on the scale is ten times stronger than the one below it. So an earthquake that measures 2 on the Richter scale

Vo•cab•u•lar•y

epicenter (ep•i•sen•tur)— the place on Earth's surface directly over where an earthquake began

is 10 times as strong as an earthquake measuring 1. An earthquake at 3 is 10 times stronger than at 2. Can you even imagine the strength of a magnitude-8 earthquake?

Another scale for measuring the strength of an earthquake is called the Modified Mercalli Scale. This scale is named after Giuseppe Mercalli [joo•**zep**•pee mehr•**kah**•lee], an Italian. His scale is based on what people see and feel during an earthquake. So the Mercalli scale is not based on sensitive instruments. It is based on people's experiences during the quake. The chart on page 100 shows how the two scales compare.

Strategy

Clarify Understanding by using photographs, charts, and other graphics to help me understand what I'm reading.

Write notes on your own paper to tell how you used this strategy.

Often, the worst damage happens in areas near the water. As the ground shakes, something strange happens in the soil. The soil may begin to be watery. This process is called **liquefaction**. Buildings, walls, wharves—anything built on this soil—may collapse and even sink part way into the ground. During the most powerful earthquakes, the ground sometimes looks like it has turned to water, and it begins to have waves! After the shaking stops, the soil goes back to the way it was.

In areas where earthquakes are common, buildings will collapse easily if they are not built right. For example, the foundations must rest on solid rock to keep the buildings from being destroyed by any liquefaction. Unlike older buildings, new buildings built according to the newest safety codes will survive with little or no damage.

Quakes measuring 1 or 2 on the Richter scale are hardly felt at all. Quakes measuring from 3 to 5 are easily felt. They may cause damage. Any quake above 6 on the scale is a major earthquake. It will likely cause damage.

The strength of an earthquake is greater as you get closer to the epicenter. The farther away you get, the less its strength.

The type of soil in the area affects the amount of damage by an earthquake. So does the way buildings are built.

The 1906 San Francisco earthquake was one of the worst on record. It was felt over 375,000 square miles. This is more than twice the size of California. There was a huge fire that followed the quake. It destroyed 28,000 buildings in the city. More than 3,000 people died from the earthquake and fire.

Vo•**cab**•u•lar•y

liquefaction
(lik•wuh•**fak**•shun)—
the process of becoming a liquid

Modified Mercalli Scale	Description	Richter Scale (Magnitude or energy released)
I	Very few people feel the earthquake.	1–2
II	On upper floors of tall buildings, people may feel it.	2–3
III	Indoors, people feel it. It feels similar to vibrations caused by passing traffic.	3–4
IV	Indoors, people feel it. Few people outdoors feel it. Windows rattle.	4
V	Nearly everyone feels it. At night, sleeping people are awakened. Some dishes and windows are broken.	4–5
VI	Everyone feels it. It is difficult to stand. Some heavy furniture moves.	5–6
VII	Some walls fall or are cracked. Everyone runs outdoors. People driving cars notice it. There is only slight damage to well-built structures.	6
VIII	There is some damage to buildings, and chimneys fall. Heavy furniture is overturned. Many people panic.	6–7
IX	Ground is noticeably cracked. There are collapsed houses and broken pipes.	7
X	Ground is badly cracked. Many buildings are destroyed. There are landslides.	7–8
XI	Few structures are standing. Bridges and railroads are destroyed.	8
XII	This is a terrible earthquake. The land looks like liquid with rolling waves. Objects are thrown into the air.	8 or greater

Earthquakes can't be stopped. But scientists are learning more about them. This new information is helping people. They can build stronger buildings. These new buildings will last through a big quake. This will save lives as well as property.

Think About the

Strategy

AFTER READING

Respond
by drawing logical conclusions about the topic.

Write notes on your own paper to tell how you used this strategy.

Vocabulary

Roots From Greek

A **root** is the main part of a word. Many Greek roots are the basis for some English words. Knowing the meaning of the Greek roots can help you find the meaning of new words. Here are two Greek roots: *seismos* means "earthquake" and *graphos* means "to write."

In this passage from "And the Earth Shakes," there is a word with both *seismos* and *graphos*.

> *Scientists have found a way to measure earthquakes. They measure how hard the shaking is. They do this with a* **seismograph.**

Use your knowledge of the Greek roots *seismos* and *graphos* to predict what the word *seismograph* means. From the Greek roots, you know that a *seismograph* has something to do with earthquakes and writing. When you read on, the passage then describes a *seismograph*. Check your prediction as you read.

> *A* **seismograph** *can measure even tiny earthquake tremors many miles away. It contains a roll of paper. The paper turns on a drum. A pen traces a line onto the paper.*

If you predicted that a **seismograph** is an instrument that measures the strength of earthquakes by writing a line on paper, the passage confirmed your prediction.

This chart shows more Greek roots and their meanings. Use the chart and words you know to identify the missing words in the phrases below. On a separate sheet of paper, write the missing root and the full word or the missing word for each item.

Greek Root	Meaning	Greek Root	Meaning
logos	study of a topic	*metron*	measure
geo	earth	*therme*	heat
seismos	earthquake		

1. scientific study of the earth   geo + ___ = ___
2. something that uses heat from inside Earth   ___ + therme = ___
3. instrument for measuring temperature   thermos + metron = ___
4. study of earthquakes   ___ + logos = ___
5. math that studies lines, angles, and shapes   geo + metron = ___

Readers' Theater

With a partner, practice performing the following script of a news interview with a survivor of an earthquake. When you are ready, perform the script for an audience.

> Try to make your voices take on the personalities of the reporter and Jacob. Read the part of the Channel 3 reporter in a concerned and serious way. Read the part of Jacob in an excited and nervous way.

Channel 3 Evening News:
Earthquake Shakes Treeville

Channel 3 Reporter: This just in. An earthquake rattled Treeville County at 6:30 PM. The earthquake measured 4.5 on the Richter scale. The earthquake's epicenter was in the area of a farm north of Treeville Center. There was only light damage in town. Let's look at this live footage from Chopper 3. As you can see, trees and power lines are down on some streets. The police reported only one injury. A heavy pot fell on a cook in Dot's Diner. He is being treated at the hospital for some bruising and dizziness. People living in the county are becoming used to earthquakes. There have been 6 earthquakes here in the past 2 years. Jacob Hale is a student at Treeville Elementary School. He is here to share his story. Jacob, what were you doing at 6:30 this evening?

Jacob: I was doing my homework. Suddenly, the books started jumping around on the desk. It was crazy!

Channel 3 Reporter: Did you know what was happening?

Jacob: Oh, yeah. I've been through lots of earthquakes. This one was stronger than any of the others, though.

Channel 3 Reporter: What did you do?

Jacob: I climbed under the desk until the tremors stopped.

Channel 3 Reporter: Officials warn that there could be more tremors this evening. So follow Jacob Hale's example. Duck for cover when you feel the ground shaking!

This has been a special report of Channel 3 News.

Think About the Strategies

Set a Purpose

by using the title and headings to write questions that I can answer while I am reading.

Clarify Understanding

by using photographs, charts, and other graphics to help me understand what I'm reading.

Respond

by drawing logical conclusions about the topic.

 Use your own paper to jot notes to apply these Before, During, and After Reading Strategies. In this selection, you will choose when to stop, think, and respond.

And the Earth Explodes

Mt. Etna erupting in
Sicily, Italy, 1993

It had been a long, hot day of work. The boy lived near the village of Paricutín [pah•ree•koo•**teen**], in Mexico. He had been plowing all morning. He was just taking a break. But wait! What was that smoke over there? The boy got up. He went to look. What he found was amazing.

A hole had formed in the soil. Smoke was coming out of it. Later that night, hot ashes started pushing up through the hole. The next morning, the sight was even scarier. The pile of ashes had grown. It was as large as a house.

Within a week, a mound 500 feet high had formed. Within a year, it had grown into a cone-shaped mountain. Melted rock, called lava, poured out of a **crater**. Ashes kept flying out. A volcano was born.

The new volcano was named Paricutín. It was named after the village. But the village was no longer there. This brand new volcano had covered up everything.

Vo•cab•u•lar•y

crater (**kray**•tuhr)—a large dent or hollow open space in the top of a volcano

[105]

Volcanoes—More Than One Kind

Volcanoes are in many places on Earth. They helped form many of the islands and mountains that shape the earth. A volcano forms by melted rock. This rock comes from deep inside Earth's crust. It is pushed up through tunnels or cracks. It is called magma when it is below Earth's surface. It's called lava when it comes out onto the surface.

The magma builds up in caves in Earth's crust. These caves are called magma chambers. Too much pressure may build up. Then magma pushes out. It comes through tunnels that are deep within the magma chambers. It reaches the surface of Earth.

Volcanoes erupt in three different ways. Some volcanoes explode. Some are quiet. Some are intermediate (somewhere in between). The kind of volcano depends on how the magma gets out.

Exploding Volcanoes

Some of Earth's biggest explosions have been when huge volcanoes blew their tops! Over time, the crater of an explosive volcano gets filled in. Pressure from rising magma and rock builds up. Finally, only one thing can happen. The volcano blows.

These blasts are huge. They are much bigger than any bomb humans have made. They tear apart islands. They destroy towns and villages. The sound from some of the explosions is fierce. It can be heard far away. There was a huge explosion in Krakatau (krak•uh•**tow**) in 1883. It was heard 3,000 miles away!

Exploding volcanoes cause much damage. They explode suddenly, so people don't have much warning. They can't get out of the way. Huge amounts of super-hot rocks and ash

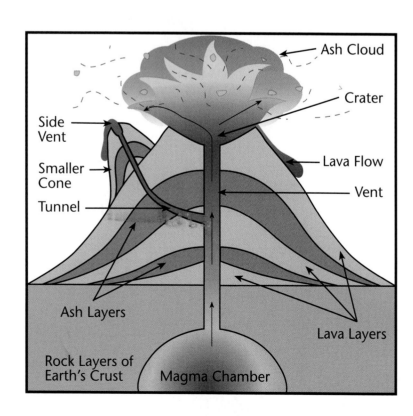

Ash Cloud

Crater

Side Vent

Smaller Cone

Tunnel

Lava Flow

Vent

Ash Layers

Lava Layers

Rock Layers of Earth's Crust

Magma Chamber

blow out. For example, Mount Pelée [puh•**lay**] is on the West Indian island of Martinique [mar•ti•**neek**]. It erupted suddenly in 1902. The mountain shook with explosions. The seaside town of St. Pierre [san pee•**air**] was smothered. A cloud of red-hot gas and ash flew out. Then they rolled down the sides of the mountains. Within 1 minute, 30,000 people died.

Mt. Pelée, Martinique

Quiet Volcanoes

Quiet volcanoes don't explode. They flow. Their craters don't get plugged up. So streams of lava just flow down their sides. The lava spreads out into broad sheets. Or it builds up into gently sloping domes. Some parts of Northern Ireland and Scotland formed this way. Lava had flowed quietly from old volcanoes.

Mount Kilauea [kee•low•**ay**•uh] on the island of Hawaii is a quiet volcano. Lava from that volcano flows for many miles. It finally pours into the ocean. As the lava flows into the colder water, it becomes solid. Lava from Mount Kilauea is slowly making the island bigger.

The lava from a quiet volcano flows slowly. So it doesn't cause much damage. There is usually plenty of time for people to leave.

Mount Kilauea, Big Island of Hawaii, 1992

They move themselves and their belongings out of the path of the lava.

Intermediate Volcanoes

Intermediate volcanoes are a little like exploding and quiet volcanoes. They may throw out the same kind of ash, rock, and gases as an explosive volcano. At other times, they erupt with quiet flows of lava. They build up cones. These hold layers of ash between layers of cooled lava. The damage caused by this volcano depends on the type of eruption.

Ruins of Pompeii, Italy

Mount Vesuvius [vi•**soo**•vee•uhs] is in Italy. It is one of the best-known intermediate volcanoes. About 2,000 years ago, Vesuvius sent a huge cloud of ash high into the sky. There was a terrific blast. Lightning flashed through the cloud of ash. The ash became so thick that it blotted out the sun.

The cloud of ash buried the Roman town of Pompeii [pom•**pay**]. It was like a blizzard of gray snow. Hundreds of people were killed. Another town was destroyed. Rain turned the layers of ash into thick mud. The mud slid down the side of Vesuvius and buried the town.

Living With Volcanoes

Many people live near volcanoes. Often, the soil on volcanic slopes is good for growing crops. Farmers think that good crops are worth the risk. In other cases, people just don't know that the mountain they are living on is a volcano. Many volcanoes don't erupt very often.

This was the case with Mount St. Helens. It is in the state of Washington. There had been more than 100 years without any explosions. The mountain suddenly erupted in 1980. The whole top of the mountain blew off. Thick clouds of ash and gas rolled down the mountain. Streams filled with the mud and ash. Not many people live in the remote area of Mount St. Helens. But sadly the blast took more than 50 lives. Many fish and wildlife were also killed.

Crater and steam—
Mount St. Helens, Washington

Geologists have a major project. It is learning to predict when a volcano is going to blow. Seismographs and other tools are placed all around active volcanoes. They record tremors. But there is a problem. Scientists still don't know what all the information means.

In the future, they hope to be able to give warnings. They will tell people that a volcano is about to erupt. Then people will be able to leave the area. They will be safe from danger.

Vo•cab•u•lar•y

geologists
(jee•**ol**•uh•juhsts)—scientists who study the earth

Words From Greek and Roman Mythology

The civilizations of ancient Greece and Rome had stories, or myths, about gods and heroes. These stories explained the natural world. Many words in English come from characters in these stories. Each character was known for a special thing. If you are familiar with the characters in the stories, you can figure out the meaning of the words that come from their names.

For example, the word *volcano* comes from Vulcan, the Roman god of fire. In "And the Earth Explodes," you learned that *volcanoes* are fiery hot mountains that push up burning ashes and magma. *Volcanoes* are like mountains on fire.

In Greek mythology, Echo was a beautiful being who could only repeat what other people said. The English word *echo* comes from her name. It means "a repetition of a sound."

On a separate sheet of paper, write the names of the Greek and Roman gods. Then use the description of each name and write the modern English word that matches it. Use a dictionary to verify your answers.

1. *Fortuna,* Roman goddess of good luck

2. *Ceres,* Roman goddess of agriculture (the process of making food)

3. *Chronos,* Greek god of time

4. *Mousa,* the goddess in Greek mythology known for her interest in song, poetry, and the arts and sciences

5. *Hygeia,* the Greek goddess of health

a. cereal

b. hygiene

c. fortune

d. chronology

e. music

Poetry

The poem below is about a volcano. Read it a few times aloud to yourself. When you think you can read it with expression and rhythm, read it aloud to others. You can also read it with a partner by alternating stanzas.

As you practice reading this poem, try to read it from the point of view of various personalities: a serious storyteller, a nervous person, a child.

Mount Peque–o

All my life I've lived beside
A place called Mount Peque–o,
But never had I any clue
It was a real volcano!

One day we heard a great big boom.
The hill began to roar.
Lava started flowing down,
And ash began to pour.

My family got away in time
But left behind our house.
It's gone the way of old Pompeii—
There was no time to douse.

So now we know our little hill
Is no ordinary mound.
There is a furnace underneath
The lava-covered ground.

Directions

How to Make a Tornado

You can make your own tornado. Read these directions and then answer the questions on the next page. You might try following the directions, too!

Things you will need:
> 2 empty 2-liter soda bottles
> water
> pinch of glitter (optional)
> 1-inch metal or plastic washer
> duct tape (or a "tornado tube" purchased at a science store)

What to do:

1 Fill one soda bottle ⅔ full of water. Add the glitter to the water.

2 Place the washer over the bottle opening. (Or twist on the tornado tube.)

3 Place the empty bottle upside down on top of the ⅔ full one. The washer will be between the two bottles.

4 Connect the bottle openings with duct tape. Wrap it tightly so no water will leak out. (Or connect the bottles with the tornado tube.)

5 Now turn the bottles upside down so the ⅔ full bottle is on top.

6 Give the bottles a twist and watch what happens.

Discussion Questions

Answer these questions with a partner or on a separate sheet of paper.

1. What does the water in the top bottle represent?

2. In this activity, what do you do after you place the washer on the filled bottle?

   a. Turn the bottle upside down.
   b. Tape the washer to the bottle.
   c. Put the glitter in the water.
   d. Put the empty bottle on top of the $^2/_3$ full one.

3. Which of these materials is not necessary for the activity?

   a. two 2-liter soda bottles
   b. water
   c. glitter
   d. 1-inch washer

4. What do you think a tornado tube does?

5. What is the purpose of the glitter?

   a. to make the water sparkle
   b. to show how tornadoes can carry objects
   c. to look like raindrops in a tornado
   d. to look like snowflakes

6. What keeps the water from just pouring from the top bottle into the bottom bottle?

7. What would happen if you turned the bottles over without twisting them?

   a. A "tornado" would not form in the top bottle.
   b. The water would not drain out of the top bottle.
   c. A "tornado" would form in the bottom bottle.
   d. The "tornado" in the top bottle would spin faster.

8. Is this a safe experiment for you to try at home? Why or why not?

EXPLORE MORE

A Tornado Plan

Pretend that a tornado is heading your way. You and your family have already set a tornado emergency plan. Explain to the class what your plan is and how you and your family go about carrying out the plan. You could do this as an oral or a written presentation.

A Diary Entry

Write a diary or a journal entry about a real or imagined tornado, earthquake, or volcano. Include specific details that show what was happening during the emergency. Tell what the writer thought about what was happening and what she or he felt, saw, and heard.

Make a Report

Choose a natural happening featured in this unit. Research information and prepare a report. It can be either oral or written, or it can be a display. This might compare the top record-setting episodes, a map showing where they took place, available data, and photographs or drawings.

Who Will Help?

Make a poster or a bulletin board display to let your class know where they can go for help if they ever need it. The Red Cross is one of many groups who work to help people after disaster strikes. Research what other groups in your area are there for help after a disaster and what they can do for the victims.

Do an Interview

Contact a disaster service team member in the area where you live. Prepare a list of questions to ask this person. Set up an appointment, and interview him or her. Be sure to record your interview or take carefully written notes of what the person says. Share your findings with the rest of your classmates.

Natural Disasters

Find out about violent weather or earth movements in the area where you live. What types of phenomena happen there? How do they affect people and property? You could present the information as an oral or a written report or as a display.

Related Books

Boekhott, P. M., and Stuart A. Kallen. *Tornadoes.* KidHaven Press, 2003.

Bourseiller, Philippe. *Volcanoes: Journey to the Crater's Edge.* H. N. Abrams, 2003.

Day, Trevor. *Guide to Savage Earth.* Dorling Kindersley Limited, 2001.

Hayhurst, Chris. *Volcanologists: Life Exploring Volcanoes.* The Rosen Publishing Group, Inc., 2003.

Heiligman, Deborah. *Earthquakes.* Scholastic, Inc., 2003.

Magloff, Lisa. *Volcano.* Dorling Kindersley Limited, 2003.

Netzley, Patricia D. *Volcanoes.* KidHaven Press, 2003.

Nicolson, Cynthia Pratt. *Tornado!* Kids Can Press, 2003.

Olien, Rebecca. *The Changing Earth.* Bridgestone Books, 2002.

Richards, Julie. *Natural Disasters: Vibrating Volcanoes.* Chelsea House Publishers, 2001.

Sakany, Lois. *Hurricane Hunters and Tornado Chasers: Life in the Eye of the Storm.* Rosen Publishing Group, Inc., 2003.

Simon, Seymour. *Danger! Volcanoes* SeaStar Books, 2002.

Tanaka, Shelley. *The Buried City of Pompeii: What It Was Like When Vesuvius Exploded.* Hyperion/Madison Press Book, 1997.

Trueit, Trudi Strain. *Earthquakes.* Franklin Watts, 2003.

—*Volcanoes.* Franklin Watts, 2003.

Zannos, Susan. *Charles Richter and the Story of the Richter Scale.* Mitchell Lane Publishers, Inc., 2004.

Interesting Web Sites

www.tornadoproject.com
www.usatoday.com/weather/wtwist0.htm
http://whyfiles.org/013tornado/index.html
www.skywarn.org/
www.nssl.noaa.gov/
http://earthquake.usgs.gov/
http://quake.wr.usgs.gov/
wwwneic.cr.usgs.gov/neis/plate_tectonics/rift_man.html
www.crustal.ucsb.edu/ics/understanding/
www.pbs.org/wnet/savageearth/earthquakes/index.html
http://volcanoes.usgs.gov/
www.pbs.org.wnet/savageearth/volcanoes/index.html
www.pbs.org.wgbh/nova/vesuvius
http://volcano.und.nodak.edu/vw.html
www.fema.gov/kids/

Unit 4
Strategies

BEFORE READING

Preview the Selection

by looking at the photographs, illustrations, captions, and graphics to predict what the selection will be about.

DURING READING

Make Connections

by comparing my experiences with what I'm reading.

AFTER READING

Recall

by using the headings to question myself about what I read.

LEARN
the **strategies**
in the selection
Mission Dietitian
page 119

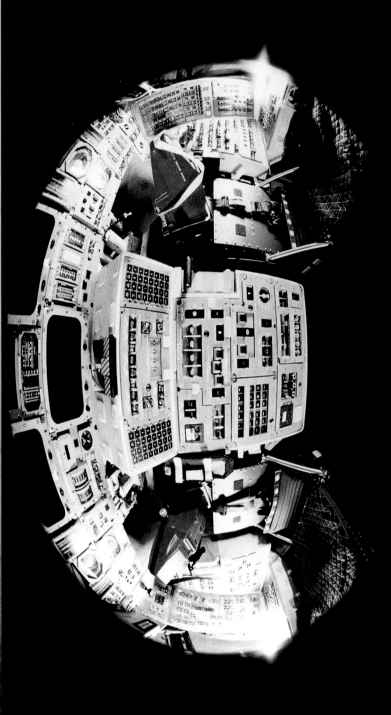

PRACTICE
the *strategies*
in the selection
Farmer on the Crew
page 131

APPLY
the *strategies*
in the selection
Space Psychologist
page 141

Think About
the
Strategies

Preview the Selection

by looking at the photographs, illustrations, captions, and graphics to predict what the selection will be about.

My Thinking

The strategy says to look at the photographs, illustrations, captions, and graphics to predict what the selection will be about.

The first two photographs show people working with food, and the captions refer to meals. The other photograph shows a man with some small plants, and the caption talks about growing plants. There's also a chart that shows sample menus for astronauts.

I predict that this selection will be about food for astronauts in space. I'll read on to see if I'm right.

Make Connections

by comparing my experiences with what I'm reading.

My Thinking

The strategy says to make connections by comparing my experiences to what I am reading. I will stop and think about this strategy every time I come to a red button like this ◉ .

Mission Dietitian

A mission specialist is organizing a meal on the mid-deck of the space shuttle *Discovery*.

Y ou tear off the end of the foil packet. You shake out the contents. A hard white lump lands on your plate. "This is ice cream?" you ask. You take a bite. "Yuck!" Now you know how our early astronauts may have felt when they ate dried ice cream.

Space food has come a long way since the ice cream astronauts ate. The meals taste much better. But someone has to figure out how to give astronauts good-tasting, healthy food. This is a very important job.

Many people are part of the food team. They range from scientists to chefs. They plan the food for space missions. And any team studying what astronauts need to eat has a **dietitian**.

Vo•**cab**•u•lar•y

dietitian (dy•i•**tish**•uhn)— a person who specializes in nutrition

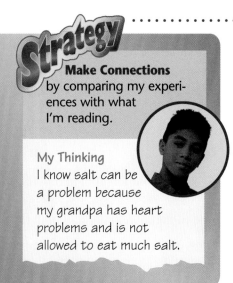
What Is a Dietitian?

A dietitian is someone who plans **nourishing** diets for people with special medical needs. Many dietitians work in hospitals. They work with doctors and other people. They make diets for patients with different needs. One patient may have to eat foods with no added salt. Another may eat only liquid foods. Such diets are very limited. Important vitamins and minerals may be missing. A dietitian knows how to replace the missing **nutrients**.

How to Become a Dietitian

Dietitians must have a college degree. They study food and nutrition. They learn about vitamins, minerals, fats, and proteins. The body needs these things to keep itself going. A dietitian must know how the body uses food. He or she must know how sickness and other medical problems can **affect** the body.

They must also study **psychology**. This helps them understand people's feelings and thoughts. These can affect what people eat. Then the dietitians can help people stay on special diets.

Vo·cab·u·lar·y

nourishing (**nur**•ish•ing)— healthful

nutrients (**noo**•tree•uhnts)— ingredients in food that nourish the body

affect (uh•**fekt**)—to make a difference in something

psychology (sy•**kol**•uh•jee)—the science that deals with how people think and act

Dietitians are working to prepare meals for space.

After college, dietitians have to work as interns for at least one year. After they serve as interns, they can work on their own. Interns often work in hospitals. They are closely **supervised**. They finish their class work. They also get hands-on experience. Then they can be **registered** in their profession as dietitians. They are ready to look for jobs, maybe with NASA.

Nutrition in Space

Astronauts are not sick. But they do have special food needs. For one thing, it is hard to cook in space. Most astronaut food is cooked ahead of time. Then it is packaged and frozen. At meal time, the food is thawed or reheated. A microwave oven onboard the space shuttle is a big help.

Each astronaut picks his or her menu with the help of a dietitian. The dietitian makes sure the astronauts get the right nutrients. Most astronauts also take vitamins and minerals in pill form. This adds to what they get from their food.

Strategy

Make Connections by comparing my experiences with what I'm reading.

My Thinking
I know about people taking vitamin pills because my brother and I both take one every day.

Astronauts must keep their bones strong. Bones stay strong on Earth because of **gravity**. In space there is no gravity. Astronauts must exercise while they are on a mission. The exercise helps keep their bones healthy. But it takes lots of energy. Astronauts must **supplement** their meals with snacks. Dietitians help decide how to add the extra food. An apple, a banana, or a handful of cashew nuts can solve the problem.

Breakfast
Hot cereal
Blueberry muffin
Cranberry juice
Milk
Coffee

Lunch
Seafood gumbo
White rice
Cole slaw
Crackers
Fruit salad
Angel food cake
Lemonade

Dinner
Green salad
(with choice of dressing)
Steak
Baked potato
  with toppings
Sautéed mushrooms
Dinner roll
Lemon pie
Tea

This is a typical space station menu for one day. It includes items the astronaut may choose to eat as a snack at a different time.

Vo·cab·u·lar·y

supervised (**soo**•puhr•vyzd)—directed and watched over

registered (**rej**•i•stuhrd)—approved to work by a professional organization

gravity (**grav**•i•tee)—the force that holds us on the earth

supplement (**sup**•luh•muhnt)—to add something to

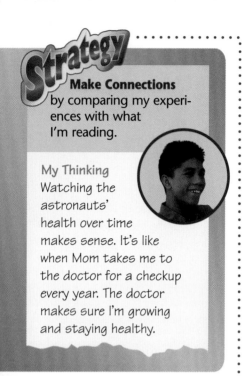

Strategy

Make Connections
by comparing my experiences with what I'm reading.

My Thinking
Watching the astronauts' health over time makes sense. It's like when Mom takes me to the doctor for a checkup every year. The doctor makes sure I'm growing and staying healthy.

Whenever the astronauts eat in space, they must be very careful. There is no gravity to hold things down. Any crumbs that get loose and start floating around inside the space vehicle can be dangerous. Also, astronauts generally use liquid salt and pepper sauces instead of the dry salt and pepper they would shake onto their food during meals on Earth. Such loose pieces could cause choking if they were breathed in. They might also get in people's eyes and cause pain and possible infections. In addition, loose particles might get into sensitive equipment and damage it.

Longer Journeys

On longer missions, dietitians may be needed as crew members. Missions to Mars, for instance, will take several years. On such a mission, the astronauts will need to stay healthy and well fed. A dietitian would watch the astronauts' health. Then he or she would make any needed changes in their diets right there in space.

This astronaut is checking some plants growing on the space shuttle *Columbia*. Much important scientific study was carried out on the *Columbia*. Sadly, this shuttle and a different crew were lost when the *Columbia* was destroyed in an accident as the vehicle was returning from space in 2003.

These two astronauts are enjoying a meal in microgravity.

Most astronauts do more than one job. The dietitian might also work as a medical specialist. He or she could run experiments. A dietitian would see how long-term space travel affects the human body. He or she might even be a pilot!

Eating in Space

Eating in space is much different from eating on Earth. On Earth, gravity holds the food—and dishes and eating utensils—in place. In **microgravity,** though, it's a different story.

Except for the International Space Station, there usually aren't any refrigerators on the space vehicles now in use. All food must be packaged so it can be stored at room temperature. This is somewhat like when you go camping here on Earth. The food you take with you can be fresh and ready-to-eat, like fruits and vegetables. Or it has to be canned, dried, or packaged to be prepared later, when you're ready to eat it.

Vo•cab•u•lar•y

microgravity
(**my**•kroh•**grav**•i•tee)—
condition of having little or no
pull of gravity

Strategy

Make Connections by comparing my experiences with what I'm reading.

My Thinking

My mom and dad kind of keep track of what my brother and I eat. They help us pick foods and snacks that are good for us. They don't like for us to eat junk food.

Food eaten in space is much the same. Each astronaut picks the foods he or she wants to eat on the trip. A dietitian makes sure the chosen foods contain enough of the required nutrients. Then the foods are prepared, packaged, and readied to make the flight.

Onboard the spacecraft, all the food is stored in the **galley**. Often, each crew member's foods are marked with a different color. When it's mealtime, the food trays are put together. Everything has to be attached to the tray. The food packages are stuck with Velcro. The silverware is attached with magnets.

Even the food has to be controlled. For example, if the crew member is eating beans or peas, the individual pieces could just float off in the cabin. But if the vegetables are in a sauce, the sauce holds them together and keeps them on the spoon until the astronaut gets them into his or her mouth. Even the straws are specially designed so they can be sealed and unsealed. Without this, drops of liquid could get loose. Any stray food or liquid that floats away could end up hurting a crew member or damaging equipment.

The food itself is in individual packages. If the food needs to be heated, it can go in a microwave oven onboard. If it needs to be **rehydrated**, special equipment in the galley is used to add the correct amount of water to the package. Depending on how much rehydrating and heating is needed, preparing a meal tray can be done in about a half hour or less.

When the crew members eat their meals and snacks, they know they are getting all the right nutrients. The dietitians and food packers figured it all out months before the spacecraft left Earth.

Blast Off!

Right now, most members of a space mission stay on the ground. It takes lots of people to get the small number of astronauts safely into orbit and back. A dietitian is one of these people. Planning the food for missions is important. Food keeps the astronauts strong and healthy. It also keeps them happy. Good meals might even keep them from being bored.

Vo·cab·u·lar·y

galley (gal•ee)—the kitchen area on a ship or spacecraft

rehydrated (ree•hy•drayt•uhd)—having the liquid put back in

In the future, more people will be moving into space. They might be on space shuttles. Or they might be on space stations. Dietitians are sure to follow. On longer missions, such as for building space colonies, dietitians will be there. They will have to make sure the food meets the needs of those people.

For now, dietitians work on the ground. They're happy to know that their work makes space travel a tasty and healthy experience!

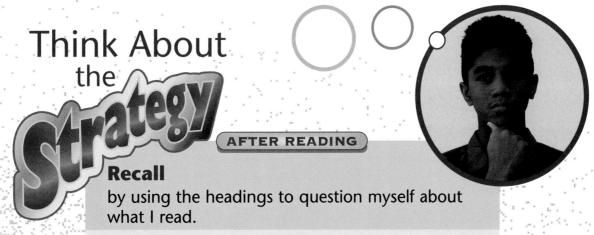

Think About the Strategy

AFTER READING

Recall
by using the headings to question myself about what I read.

My Thinking

The strategy says I should recall by using the headings to question myself about what I read. The first heading is "What Is a Dietitian?" Now I know that a dietitian is trained to plan meals for all different kinds of people.

How can I become a dietitian? I would have to go to college and study food, nutrition, and psychology. I also would have to be an intern. Then I could get my license.

What do I need to know about nutrition in space? I learned that astronauts have special food needs and must take vitamin and mineral pills. Each one designs his or her own menu of meals and snacks, with the help of a dietitian.

What will happen on longer journeys? Dietitians may need to be onboard. They would probably also have more than one job.

What was in the "Blast Off!" section? Now, dietitians don't go into space. They work on Earth to keep astronauts healthy. But they may end up going into space with crews on longer missions in the future.

Graphic organizers help us organize information. I think this article can be organized by using a Venn diagram. A Venn diagram shows features that are the same for two different things. It also shows ways the two things are different from each other. This Venn diagram compares early space food with modern space food, showing how they are different and how they are alike.

Venn Diagram
Mission Dietitian

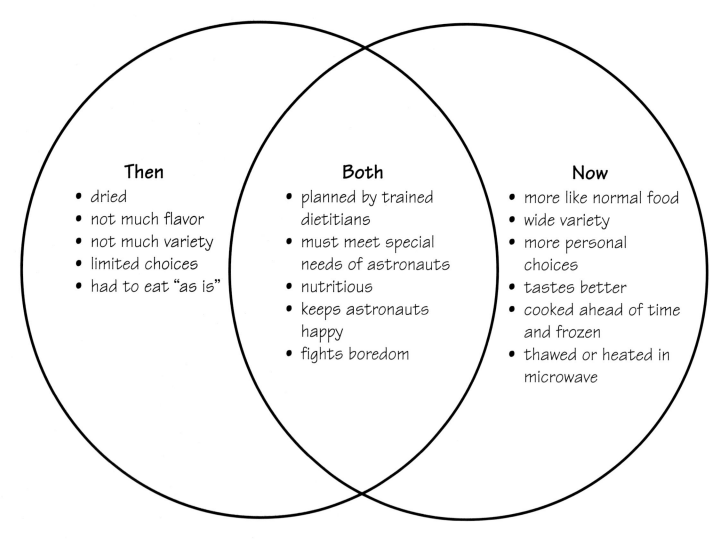

Then
- dried
- not much flavor
- not much variety
- limited choices
- had to eat "as is"

Both
- planned by trained dietitians
- must meet special needs of astronauts
- nutritious
- keeps astronauts happy
- fights boredom

Now
- more like normal food
- wide variety
- more personal choices
- tastes better
- cooked ahead of time and frozen
- thawed or heated in microwave

I used my graphic organizer to write a summary of the article. Can you find the information in my summary that came from my Venn diagram?

A Summary of
Mission Dietitian

Ever since the first astronauts went out into space, people on Earth have had to figure out how to keep them from being hungry. Astronauts still eat when they are on space missions, but the food they eat has changed a lot.

Introduction
Here is my introduction. It gives the main idea of my summary.

On the first flights into space, ice cream was not cold and delicious. It was a hard, dry lump. After the food was dried, it didn't have a lot of flavor left. Ice cream and other kinds of food were sealed in foil packets. Astronauts had few choices for their meals. They had to eat pretty much whatever was in the packets, just the way it was. They didn't even have a microwave with them! How do you think that dried food tasted?

Now astronauts eat more normal food. And they can pick from a huge list, so they can be sure to have foods they like. They can help design their own menus, too. The food looks better and tastes better. It is cooked ahead of time, packaged, and frozen. Then it is thawed. If astronauts want to heat it, they can put it into a microwave oven right there on the space shuttle.

Body
I used information from the "Then" and "Now" parts of my Venn diagram in the middle of my summary. Here, I'm telling about how space food was for the first astronauts and how it is now.

The food in space has changed, but some things have stayed the same. Dietitians still plan the astronauts' meals. These people make sure the astronauts get all the vitamins and minerals they need. Eating nearly always makes people feel good, and it helps keep them from getting bored. This is really important when the astronauts are on long stays on a space shuttle or on the space station. Still, the astronauts are much happier when their ice cream is not a dry lump!

Conclusion
I ended my paper by using information from the "Both" section of my Venn diagram. This part tells how some things have changed and how some things about space food are the same.

Synonyms

A **synonym** is a word that has the same or nearly the same meaning as another word. For example, *big* and *large* are synonyms. Read this passage from "Mission Dietitian":

*Astronauts must **supplement** their meals with snacks. Dietitians help decide how to add the extra food. An apple, a banana, or a handful of cashew nuts can solve the problem.*

In this passage, the word *supplement* is a verb that means "to add something to." *Supplement* can also be a noun that means "something added to complete another thing."

The word *complement* is a synonym of *supplement. Complement* is a noun that means "something that completes something else or makes it whole."

Read the sentences below. Notice that both *supplement* and *complement* can be used in the same place in the same sentence.

*Fruits and nuts are perfect **supplements** to an astronaut's diet. Fruits and nuts are perfect **complements** to an astronaut's diet.*

Synonyms can be found in a thesaurus. A **thesaurus** is similar to a dictionary. It lists words in alphabetical order, but it lists the synonyms and antonyms of each word instead of its meaning.

Read the following sentences. Then, on a separate sheet of paper, write at least two synonyms for each boldface word. Use a dictionary or a thesaurus if you need help.

1. My brother's grin grew wide when he **discovered** his birthday presents in the closet.
2. I **grabbed** onto the handrail when I started to slip on the icy steps.
3. Most of the students in the class thought the science test was **difficult**.
4. I am always **cautious** when I am getting off the school bus.
5. "Yes!" I **replied** when the teacher asked me if I had my permission slip.

Poetry

The three parts, or stanzas, of this poem explore the subject of space food. Practice reading the poem aloud to yourself until you become familiar with its rhythm. Then read it aloud to others.

> Notice the rhyme and rhythm pattern in each stanza. Lines 1, 2, and 5 rhyme and have a similar pattern. Lines 3 and 4 have another rhyme and rhythm pattern. Be sure that the questions in the poem sound like real questions.

Space Food

What is the food like in space?
Does the food have any taste?
It must have nutrition,
On every mission.
The food must not go to waste.

So what do astronauts eat?
Do they get anything sweet?
Dried or frozen,
Good foods are chosen.
Meals are always complete.

Food can't be hard to prepare.
It might be floating in air.
If it's easy and neat,
And comes with a treat,
The crew won't have a care!

Think About
the
Strategies

BEFORE READING

Preview the Selection

by looking at the photographs, illustrations, captions, and graphics to predict what the selection will be about.

 Write notes on your own paper to tell how you used this strategy.

DURING READING

Make Connections

by comparing my experiences with what I'm reading.

 When you come to a red button like this , write notes on your own paper to tell how you used this strategy.

Farmer on the Crew

Spinach salad with fresh tomatoes and mushrooms

The spaceship captain stands next to a special opening. She speaks. "Spinach salad. With tomatoes." Seconds later, a **china** bowl filled with salad takes shape in the opening. Even a fork appears. The captain takes out the bowl and fork and tastes the spinach. She walks away as if this were a common event.

Computers in science fiction movies and shows are able to make food appear out of thin air. In real life, though, it doesn't work this way. Food still has to be packed and put aboard the spaceship before it leaves the ground. Food still comes to us the old-fashioned way. It comes from plants and animals, not from computers.

Vo•cab•u•lar•y

china (**chy**•nuh)—a kind of fine white pottery

Food in Space

Someday, people may be living on a space station. Or they may be traveling on a long trip to Mars. Having fresh food aboard will be one of their biggest problems. Growing food onboard the spacecraft is one **solution**. Russian crews have grown vegetables on their space stations. They enjoyed eating their own space-grown tomatoes. Someday, gardeners and farmers may be important members of space mission crews.

Fresh Food

Freshly grown food is important. As soon as a fruit or vegetable is picked, it begins to lose nutrients. At each step in the **processing** of the food, more nutrients are lost. Processing food means boxing it, storing it, cooking it, and canning it. Many nutrients are lost when food is processed. One **stage** of the processing may be putting the nutrients back in.

Vo•cab•u•lar•y

solution (suh•loo•shuhn)—a way of solving a problem

processing (pros•es•ing)—series of steps taken to prepare or preserve something

stage (stayj)—a step in a process

Astronaut Shannon W. Lucid checks the progress of a wheat growth experiment on Russia's *Mir* Space Station.

[132]

Also, many people think that fresh food tastes better. Having fresh food would be valuable on space flights or space stations. Growing food right on the spot would improve its taste and nutritional value. It would also mean that large amounts of food would not have to be carried from Earth to a space station or colony.

Strategy

Make Connections by comparing my experiences with what I'm reading.

Write notes on your own paper to tell how you used this strategy.

A plant growth chamber aboard one of the flights of the space shuttle *Columbia* helped scientists study the growth of plants in space. Much important scientific research was carried out on the *Columbia*.

Growing Plants in Space

Growing food plants in space does not mean just pushing seeds down into soil, watering them, and waiting for the plants to sprout. Plants that grow on Earth respond to the way things are on Earth. In space, Earth-like conditions have to be set up for plants to grow. Plants are used to Earth's sunlight and air. They need these to make food. Sunlight on Earth comes through Earth's **atmosphere**.

Vo·cab·u·lar·y

atmosphere
(**at**·muh·sfeer)—air

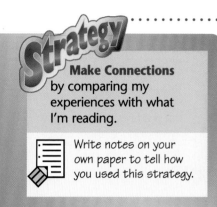
The atmosphere surrounds Earth. It lets in some kinds of light and screens out others. Space gardeners will need special light bulbs to supply the right kind of light for plants. They will also need pots filled with a mixture of gases that is like the air on Earth.

Gravity

Plants are used to Earth's gravity. It makes their roots grow down into the soil. In space, there is no gravity, so there is no "up" or "down." Therefore, plant roots in space do not know which way to grow. Scientists on the space shuttle found that spinning the potted plants helps their roots find "down." Plants that are placed in spinning containers grow better. One task of a space farmer might be to keep plant containers spinning in space.

Soil

Plants on Earth get water and nutrients from the soil. Soil is another problem for space flights. Soil is heavy. Spacecraft are designed to be as light as possible. The lighter they are, the easier it is to get them into space.

One solution to this problem is called **hydroponics**. Hydroponics is a way of growing plants in a small amount of special liquid instead of soil. The liquid gives the plants all the water and nutrients they would normally get from soil. The plant stems usually grow through a screen or mesh. This holds them up while their roots float in the liquid. Lamps shine on their leaves. This gives the right amount of light. A space farmer would need to mix just the right liquid for each plant. He or she would add the right nutrients to make sure the plants thrive.

Once astronaut crews reach their far-off destination and get set up on the surface of their new home, they can begin to plant crops. Several different food plants probably could be raised. After the crops are raised and harvested, they will have to be processed into a form the astronauts can eat. For example, the wheat will have to be ground into flour. Then the flour can be used to make bread. The grinding and baking might be done on the space vehicle.

Vo•cab•u•lar•y

hydroponics (hy•druh•**pon**•iks)—growing plants in a liquid instead of in soil

Food Crops Astronauts Might Grow

- potatoes
- carrots
- radishes
- wheat
- peanuts
- soybeans
- dried beans
- quinoa
- lettuce
- spinach
- tomatoes
- herbs
- cabbage
- rice

Farming in Space

Astronauts may someday set foot on a far-off place such as Mars. Before that happens, though, much planning has to be done. Scientists are already testing possible solutions for the problem of having enough food supplies.

Mars has no air or water. A kind of **greenhouse** will have to be set up on the surface of the planet. The greenhouse will give shelter from temperature highs and lows. It will also be equipped to keep the plants watered. It will give them the right light for growing. Possible greenhouse designs are being tested.

Vo·cab·u·lar·y

greenhouse
(**green**•hows)—a special container for growing and protecting plants

[135]

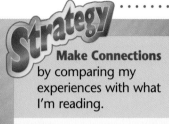

NASA has been testing a special greenhouse. They set it up on Devon Island, in northern Canada. Conditions on the island are severe. Winter temperatures are very cold. The island is like a desert. There is a huge ice field at one end of it. Of course, these conditions are not just like on Mars. But they are similar in some ways. The greenhouse lets scientists set up experiments to grow plants from seed. Then they can check growth results in the special growing area.

One other area on Earth might be a good site for testing Mars-like conditions. This is the Atacama Desert in South America. This desert is probably the driest place on Earth. It receives about one tenth of an inch of rain—every few years. This might be another good place to test a greenhouse. It would have to supply its own moisture.

This NASA photo of the landscape on Mars shows conditions the first visitors there will face.

Scientists are also testing and developing several kinds of seeds. For space farming, seeds will have to grow quickly. And the plants must take up as small a space as possible. For example, typical wheat plants on Earth are about 18 inches tall when the wheat is ripe. A new dwarf wheat plant, however, is different. It is about 12 inches tall when it is ready to harvest. "Fast plant" seeds would be needed. They would enable the farmer on Mars to harvest food much faster than is possible using regular plant seeds.

Much planning and testing must be done before astronauts will be doing any real farming in space. But someday, we may be reading news reports about the first food crops on Mars.

Salad for Supper

Remember how the salad was "made" in the first paragraph? Here is a more realistic space salad. The space station gardener opens the hatch into the crew's quarters. Over his arm is a basket filled with leafy green spinach and bright red tomatoes. "Here's today's harvest!" he calls.

The astronauts gather around. One of them picks up a tomato and smells it.

"Yum, sliced tomatoes tonight! The food out here is great."

The gardener grins.

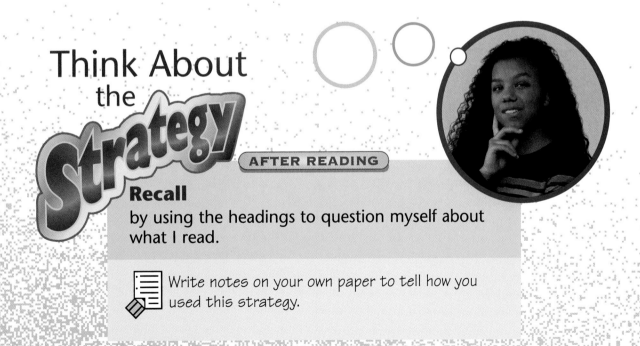

Think About the Strategy

AFTER READING

Recall
by using the headings to question myself about what I read.

Write notes on your own paper to tell how you used this strategy.

Vocabulary

Word Origins: Toponyms

Some words in English come from the names of places. These words are called **toponyms**.

Here is an example of a toponym from "Farmer on the Crew":

> *The spaceship captain stands next to a special opening. She speaks. "Spinach salad. With tomatoes." Seconds later, a **china** bowl filled with salad takes shape in the opening.*

The word *china* means "a kind of fine white pottery." This type of pottery originally came from China. How do you know when *china* means "pottery" and when it means "the country"? There are two ways:

1. Look for a capital letter at the beginning of the name of a place.

2. Use context clues. The word *bowl* is a clue that *china* means "pottery" in this sentence.

Many food words are named after the places they came from. Read the clues below. Then try to think of the food word and the name of the place the food comes from. Write your answers on a separate sheet of paper. Use an atlas or a map of Europe if you need help.

1. You might call it a hot dog, but that's not its original name. This sausage is a favorite at baseball games. It is named after a town in Germany. Clue: f _ _ _ _ f u r t e r

2. People eat this meat patty on a bun with ketchup. It is also named after a town in Germany.
Clue: _ _ m b _ _ _ _ _

3. This lunch food is made of two pieces of bread with something in the middle. It is named for the earl of a town in England. Clue: _ _ _ _ w _ c h

4. A kind of fancy mustard was originally made in a certain town in France. Clue: _ _ j o n

5. This hard cheese is sometimes described as "sharp." Other times it is described as "New York," even though it comes from a town in England. Clue: _ _ _ d d _ _

Readers' Theater

The space dietitian and the space farmer know a lot about food, plants, and nutrition. They must work together to solve a problem. Practice reading this script with a partner. When you and your partner are ready, present the script to others.

This script is a conversation between two experts in their fields. As you practice this script, try to make your reading sound like a real conversation. Try to make your voice show knowledge and authority.

Space Dietitian: We are here to solve a problem. How can astronauts have healthy, fresh food to eat while they are on long space missions?

Space Farmer: I think that, together, we can find a solution. What kinds of foods do astronauts need?

Space Dietitian: Our goal is to grow fresh vegetables and fruits. Grains and proteins can be dried or frozen, so they are easier to pack.

Space Farmer: So you would like to grow plants in space, right?

Space Dietitian: Yes, I think that would be a good solution.

Space Farmer: Plants need sunlight. We could use special light bulbs that act like the sun.

Space Dietitian: Wonderful! But plants need soil, too. That could be a problem. Soil is too heavy. A spacecraft must be light, or it will use too much fuel getting into orbit.

Space Farmer: We could grow the plants in a small amount of water. It's a special method called hydroponics.

Space Dietitian: Amazing! But what will happen to the plants' roots? Without gravity, they won't know which way to grow.

Space Farmer: If something is spinning or turning, it acts like there is gravity. So we will need to keep the plants turning. Then the roots will grow down into the water.

Space Dietitian: Terrific! The astronauts will be able to grow their own fresh food. On a long mission, they will always have something fresh and nutritious to eat.

Space Farmer: Problem solved! Future astronauts will enjoy their own fresh food.

Think About
the

BEFORE READING

Preview the Selection

by looking at the photographs, illustrations, captions, and graphics to predict what the selection will be about.

DURING READING

Make Connections

by comparing my experiences with what I'm reading.

AFTER READING

Recall

by using the headings to question myself about what I read.

 Use your own paper to jot notes to apply these Before, During, and After Reading Strategies. In this selection, you will choose when to stop, think, and respond.

Space Psychologist

Getting from one part of a space vehicle to another can be a tight squeeze.

Imagine that it's day 411 of the 1,000-day space journey to Titan. Many long days lie ahead. One crew member has not been coping well. Finally, the crew member snaps. "I can't stand it anymore. I want to get off this ship!"

Another crew member comes up. She says quietly, "I'd like to talk with you." The second crew member might be the ship's psychologist.

What Is a Psychologist?

A **psychologist** is a doctor who studies how people feel and behave. Psychologists have to go to college. Then they study for several more years. There is much that they need to know.

Most psychologists are curious about people. They want to know why we do what we do. Some of them study how humans act. They carry out **research**. They do **experiments**. Others work as **counselors**. Their knowledge is important. They help people deal with their problems. The space program uses both kinds of doctors.

On the Ground

Psychologists do important work before a space flight ever gets off the ground. They find out what types of people will make the best astronauts. Some space shuttles stay in space for one or two weeks at a time.

A small place is crammed with lots of people and equipment. There's not much privacy. You may want some time to yourself. But you can't just go out for a walk.

What type of person will work best in space? The doctors study this question. What they learn is used to help select astronauts.

Qualities and Skills Common to Most Astronauts

✔ Strong skills in math, science, and communication

✔ Strong leadership skills

✔ Good citizenship (understanding and appreciating ethnic and cultural differences, American history, and current events)

✔ Fluency in at least two languages

✔ Being a team player

✔ Higher education (at least a bachelor's degree)

✔ Adaptability and motivation (able and willing to try new and challenging things)

Vo·cab·u·lar·y

psychologist (sy•**kol**•uh•jist)— a doctor trained in how people think and behave

research (ri•**surch**)—careful study

experiments (ik•**sper**•uh•muhnts)—tests or trials to learn the truth about something

counselors (**kown**•suh•luhrz)—advisers

Testing Astronaut Candidates

The doctors use special tests for astronaut **candidates**. They find out if people who want to be astronauts are suited to space travel. Some of the tests are paper and pencil tests. Others are done in **interviews**. Still others are done in a group setting.

The doctors study each candidate. They watch how he or she deals with other people in the group. Then they use these tests to get a clear picture of each person.

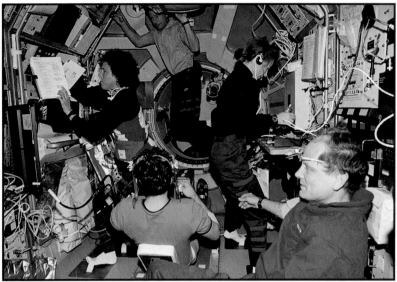

Astronauts are working in the space shuttle cargo bay of *Atlantis*.

Preparing Astronauts for Space

Before going into space, astronauts receive briefings from many people. A briefing is a detailed talk about some part of a mission. Astronauts are briefed on the jobs they are to do. For example, they might practice all the steps for running the space shuttle. They must work under normal conditions. But they also must be prepared for emergencies.

They get briefings from doctors. Other astronauts also brief them. These people tell them what to expect. They learn ways to deal with being cooped up in a tiny space. They learn how to cope without losing their temper.

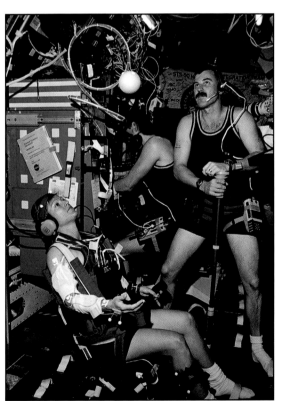

Astronauts are tested to see how they will respond to certain conditions in space.

Vo•cab•u•lar•y

candidates (**kan**•di•dayts)— people who are trying to receive a special award or honor

interviews (**in**•tuhr•vyooz)— face-to-face meetings to talk about something special

Astronauts must stick to the plan for the mission. They follow orders from Mission Control. The doctors discuss how individuals can play down their own **goals**. They must focus on the goals of the mission.

Out in Space

Someday doctors may go with space crews. They can help crew members cope with long or difficult missions. Their studies will be helpful in choosing people for such missions. They will help crews work well together.

Think of a long space mission, such as a journey to Mars. Doctors may be onboard. The space shuttle will be far from Earth. It's hard to know how people will act on long flights. Problems will come up. But they will have to be solved by the crew itself. Getting help from Earth will take too long.

The psychologist will watch how different people act. This is much like a doctor watching how their bodies respond. The psychologist will know ways to help the crew stay mentally healthy. Then they can do the jobs they need to do. They will carry out the goals of the mission.

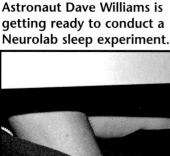

Astronaut Dave Williams is getting ready to conduct a Neurolab sleep experiment.

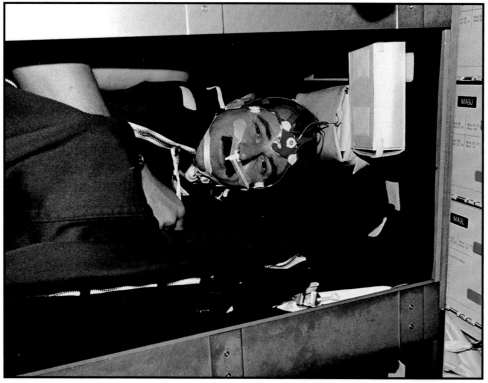

Planning for Long Missions

Will people who are quiet and private do well on a long mission? Or will people who are outgoing and social do better? Who will do best under the stress of long missions? Doctors study these questions. They study reports of people who have been in similar places, such as on submarines.

Vo·cab·u·lar·y

goals (gohlz)—purposes or aims

Doctors may ask volunteers to simulate being on a long space flight. *Simulate* means "to create the same conditions as closely as possible." Doctors will study how people react to the **confinement,** boredom, loneliness, and fear they might face in space.

Psychologists also study how new ideas might affect the crew. For example, would it help if members had videos of family and friends with them on the flight? In a test, some groups would have videos. Others would not. Doctors would compare the reactions of these two groups. They could then suggest ways to make space flight as pleasant as possible.

Space Psychology and the Future

In the future, psychologists will do much research. They will have lots of questions to ask the first ones who return from long missions. Did the doctors' plans and advice help the astronauts? Were there any surprises? From the answers will come new plans for future space travel.

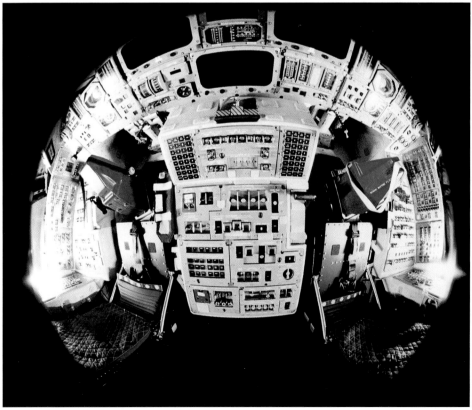

Control panel of a space vehicle

Vo·**cab**·u·lar·y

confinement
(kuhn•**fyn**•muhnt)—quality of being shut in or having limited freedom

Word Parts

Some words are made of many parts. When you know the meaning of the parts, you can find the meaning of the word. Read this passage from "Space Psychologist."

Psychologists do important work before a space flight ever gets off the ground. They find out what types of people will make the best astronauts. Some space shuttles stay in space for one or two weeks at a time.

The word *astronaut* is made up of the word parts *astro* and *naut*. In Greek, *astro* means "star" and *naut* means "sailor." What do "star" and "sailor" tell you about the word *astronaut*? You could say that an *astronaut* sails among the stars.

Use the definition of the word part *naut* to match the word on the left with its definition on the right. Write your answers on a separate piece of paper. Then use a dictionary to check your answers.

1. aeronaut (clue: *aero-* means "air")

2. cosmonaut (clue: *cosmo-* means "universe")

3. aquanaut (clue: *aqua-* means "water")

4. Argonaut (clue: Argo is a large group of stars.)

5. nautilus (clue: This word is from a Greek word that means "sailor.")

a. a person who is on a dangerous but rewarding mission

b. a scuba diver who operates equipment or works underwater for a period of time

c. an animal that lives in the ocean

d. the pilot of a blimp or balloon

e. a Russian space traveler

Interview

Here is a fictional interview. Katie Chen is an astronaut. She just returned from a month-long mission on a space station. Andrew Garcia is a psychologist. He is interviewing Chen, asking her how she liked the experience. With a partner, practice reading the interview. When you are ready, read the script to others.

TIP

The person playing the part of Andrew Garcia should read the script in a calm and serious way. Be sure to make the questions Garcia asks sound like real questions.

A Psychologist Interviews an Astronaut

Garcia: How did it feel to live on a space station?

Chen: It was exciting! The views of Earth were amazing. But there was a lot to do. There wasn't much time to relax and enjoy it.

Garcia: That must have been exciting! Did you wish you had more relaxation time?

Chen: Actually, I liked being busy. When I had nothing to do, I started to miss being at home.

Garcia: And home was far away, down on Earth. What did you miss most about home?

Chen: I missed my husband and kids the most. I also missed being outside. I missed the sun and even the rain!

Garcia: How did you find the living quarters on the space station?

Chen: It was very cramped. I slept on a narrow bunk. Six of us shared the same sleeping quarters. Sometimes I wanted to be alone. But there was no place to go.

Garcia: Did you ever feel afraid during your mission?

Chen: I knew that it was a very safe mission. But every astronaut has fears. Sometimes I worried as I was falling asleep.

Garcia: I think I would have been afraid. Do you want to go on another space mission?

Chen: Absolutely! Being out in space was the experience of a lifetime.

Charts

Getting Food Ready for Space

Food is prepared for the astronauts in different ways. Here are some of them. Notice the abbreviations.

FF   **Fresh Food:** food just as it is grown. Example: apples.

IM   **Intermediate Moisture:** food that has had some water taken out of it. This food is still soft and can be eaten as it is. Example: dried peaches.

NF   **Natural Form:** food that is ready to eat. Examples: nuts, cookies.

R   **Rehydratable:** food that has all the water removed. Water must be added before this food can be eaten. Example: oatmeal.

T   **Thermostabilized:** food that has been heated to preserve it. This food is stored in cans or packaged in plastic cups. Example: tuna fish.

Look over these charts of fruits and vegetables. Notice how the foods are prepared for space flights.

Fruits	Preparation
Apple	FF
Applesauce	T
Apricots, Dried	IM
Banana	FF
Orange	FF
Peach Ambrosia	R
Peaches, Diced	T
Peaches, Dried	IM
Pears, Diced	T
Pears, Dried	IM
Pineapple	T
Strawberries	R
Trail Mix	IM

Vegetables	Preparation
Asparagus	R
Broccoli au Gratin	R
Carrot Sticks	FF
Cauliflower w/Cheese	R
Celery Sticks	FF
Green Beans and Broccoli	R
Green Beans and Mushrooms	R
Italian	R
Spinach, Creamed	R
Tomatoes and Eggplant	T

Discussion Questions

Answer these questions with a partner or on a separate sheet of paper.

1. Which food on the list needs to have water added before you can eat it?
   a. apple
   b. diced pears
   c. carrot sticks
   d. green beans and broccoli

2. List two foods that are dried a little but can be eaten as they are.

3. What do astronauts do after they open a package of strawberries?

4. Read the definitions for ways to prepare food. What do you think the word part *thermo-* means?
   a. water
   b. heat
   c. cold
   d. dried

5. Choose four foods from the lists that are served the same on Earth and in space.

6. Think about the food you eat at home. Which of these has been thermostabilized?
   a. corn in cans
   b. eggs in cartons
   c. potatoes in bags
   d. a head of lettuce

7. How can research on ways to prepare food for the astronauts help us here on Earth?
   a. We will learn how to prepare food for astronauts.
   b. We will learn better ways to preserve food.
   c. We will not have to eat dried ice cream.
   d. More people will want to be astronauts.

8. Is the food that astronauts eat becoming more like ours—or more different from ours? Explain your answer.

EXPLORE MORE

Research Hydroponic Gardening

Collect the necessary supplies for a hydroponic garden, and set up a small container for growing some simple plants, such as tomatoes, lettuce, or cucumbers. Place the container where classmates can observe the growing process.

Making a Food Log

Keep a food log for at least three days. Record the food you eat and the time you eat it. Research nutrition information to figure out if the vitamins and minerals in the food are adequate for a healthy diet. Decide what changes you may need to make to improve the nutrition level of your diet.

Interview the Crew

Pretend that you are a reporter preparing to interview the crew returning from Earth's first space mission to Mars. Write a list of questions you want the crew to answer. Be sure to include a variety of topics, touching on the make-up of the crew, daily life aboard the spacecraft, experiences of deep-space travel, overcoming fear, boredom and loneliness, scientific accomplishments, and any others you think are important.

Writing a Diary or Journal

Imagine being on a long-term space mission. Write a series of diary or journal entries that tell about such things as physical condition, mood, and general attitude. Describe daily activities and how these are carried out within the limitations of the traveling space vehicle and the conditions onboard while you are in deep space.

Need a Job?

Think of a job you might like to do for NASA or another space organization. Do research to learn what the requirements are for the job.

Record an Interview

Make a video or audio recording of an interview. Have a small group of friends imagine they are the crew just returning from Earth's first space mission to Mars. Use a list of questions from the previous activity and interview the crew. Encourage them to focus on details in a variety of activities and experiences. Present the recording to the rest of the class.

Related Books

Becklake, Sue. *100 Things You Should Know About Space.* Mason Crest Publishers, 2003.

Bredeson, Carmen. *Living on a Space Shuttle.* Children's Press, 2003.

Briggs, Carole S. *Women in Space.* Lerner Publications Company, 1999.

Challoner, Jack. *The Atlas of Space.* Copper Beech Books, 2001.

Furniss, Tim. *The Atlas of Space Exploration.* Michael Friedman Publishing Group, Inc., 2002.

Glatzer, Jenna. *The Exploration of the Moon.* Mason Crest Publishers, 2003.

Goodman, Susan E. *Ultimate Field Trip 5: Blasting Off to Space Academy.* Atheneum Books for Young Readers, 2001.

Graham, Ian. *You Wouldn't Want to Be on Apollo 13!: A Mission You'd Rather Not Go On.* Franklin Watts, 2003.

Pentland, Peter, and Pennie Stoyles. *Space Science.* Chelsea House Publishers, 2003.

Richie, Jason. *Space Flight: Crossing the Last Frontier.* The Oliver Press, Inc., 2002.

Siy, Alexandra. *Footprints on the Moon.* Charlesbridge Publishing, 2001.

Walker, Niki. *The Life of an Astronaut.* Crabtree Publishing Company, 2001.

Interesting Web Sites

Learn more about the history of space travel and about what's going on today in the field of space exploration.

http://www.kidsastronomy.com/fun/index.htm

http://www.spacekids.com/

http://www.gomilpitas.com/homeschooling/explore/astronomy.htm

http://www.frontiernet.net/~kidpower/astronomy.html

http://liftoff.msfc.nasa.gov/

http://www.jsc.nasa.gov/people/justforkids.html

http://www.kidsastronomy.com/news.htm

http://www.kennedyspacecenter.com/html/just_for_kids.html

http://lsda.jsc.nasa.gov/kids/L&W/livework.htm

http://origin.mars5.jpl.nasa.gov/gallery/

Web sites have been carefully researched for accuracy, content, and appropriateness. However, teachers and caregivers are reminded that Web sites are subject to change. Internet use should always be monitored.

Unit 5

Strategies

BEFORE READING

Activate Prior Knowledge
by reading the introduction and/or summary to decide what I know about this topic.

DURING READING

Interact With Text
by identifying how the text is organized.

AFTER READING

Evaluate
by forming a judgment about whether the selection was objective or biased.

LEARN
the **strategies**
in the selection
Bringing East and West Together
page 155

PRACTICE
the *strategies*
in the selection
The Orphan Trains
page 167

APPLY
the *strategies*
in the selection
**Whatever Happened to the
Passenger Train?**
page 177

Think About
the
Strategies

Activate Prior Knowledge

by reading the introduction and/or summary to decide what I know about this topic.

My Thinking

The strategy says to activate prior knowledge by reading the introduction and/or summary to decide what I know about this topic. I read the introduction (there isn't a summary for this one). It tells about how quick and easy it is to travel across the country now compared with how it used to be.

Back in 1850, roads were not very good. There weren't any trains, cars, or airplanes yet. Traveling long distances was hard and uncomfortable for most people. Then the steam locomotive was invented, and travel began to change. I remember a lot of that from reading books, seeing movies, and studying in school. I don't remember many of the details, though. I need to keep reading.

DURING READING

Interact With Text

by identifying how the text is organized.

My Thinking

The strategy says to interact with text by identifying how the text is organized. I will stop and think about this strategy every time I come to a red button like this ⊙.

Bringing East and West Together

Introduction

The United States seems much smaller now than it did in 1850. Today, we can fly across the country. It only takes a few hours. Or we can drive from New York to California. That can be done in a few days. We can stay in nice motels along the way.

In 1850, though, few people traveled from the East Coast to the West. The trip was too long and dangerous. There were no airplanes or cars or motels. Those would have made the trip easier. There weren't even any trains.

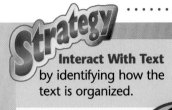
The "roads" were bumpy dirt paths. People traveled slowly. They went by horse. Or they drove covered wagons.

Back then, ships were a good choice. They carried heavy loads, such as lumber. But ships could go only where the rivers went.

The steam locomotive was invented in 1850. Then trains could go anywhere there were tracks. By 1854, railroad tracks reached from the Atlantic Coast to the Mississippi River. But many people wanted more. They were eager to settle the land beyond the Mississippi. Businessmen began to plan. They wanted tracks all the way to the West Coast.

Getting Started

In 1862, President Lincoln signed the Railroad Act. It set the stage for the first cross-country railroad. The Union Pacific Railroad Company would start laying tracks in Omaha, Nebraska. It would move west.

The Central Pacific Railroad Company would start in Sacramento, California. It would move east. They would meet in Utah. There, the two tracks would connect. They would become one railroad.

The Chinese Contribute

The Civil War stopped the project until 1865. Not long after the war ended, a race began. Each railroad company wanted to win. Each hoped to lay more track than the other. This was because the government paid so well. It paid for each mile of track. The companies also got huge areas of land along the track they laid.

Both companies had a problem, though. They couldn't find enough men for the hard work. At that time, not many people lived in California. The Central Pacific Railroad took a chance. It hired some Chinese **immigrants**. "The Chinese are too small," some people warned. "They're not strong enough!"

Yet the Chinese were soon at work. They were laying track faster and straighter than the other workers. In no time, almost every Chinese man in California was working for the railroad. Nearly 80 percent of the Central Pacific workers were Chinese.

Vo·cab·u·lar·y

immigrants (im·i·gruhnts)— persons who come from one country to live permanently in another country

[156]

The workers lived on a train. It followed them down the track they had just laid. The train pulled boxcars with built-in bunks. It also had a "chuck wagon" car. This is where meals were cooked. More cars carried lumber, rails, **spikes,** and other supplies.

Working From East to West

The Union Pacific workers laid about a mile of track a day. They were working across the Great Plains. They each earned $2 a day. Sometimes they could lay an extra half-mile of track. Then they were paid $3!

The workers suffered in **blizzards**. These storms often swept across the plains. They also faced angry Plains Indians. These Native Americans were afraid. They knew the railroad would help end their way of life.

In fact, the government was giving away land. But the land belonged to the Native Americans. To protect the workers, the government sent the **cavalry**. They often shot any Indians they saw.

This early photograph shows railroad workers on the job.

Vo·cab·u·lar·y

spikes (spyks)—very large nails

blizzards (bliz•urdz)—long, severe snowstorms

cavalry (kav•uhl•ree)— an army group on horseback

Strategy

Interact With Text
by identifying how the text is organized.

My Thinking

Work began soon after the Civil War ended in 1865. Workers were digging tunnels during the winter of 1867. In the section before this one, I read about the Union Pacific progress. Now I'm reading about the Central Pacific work that was being done during the same time period. I was right. The text is following a time order.

Working From West to East

The Central Pacific crews worked more slowly. They faced a huge wall—the Sierra Mountains! They used picks and shovels. They made tunnels into the rock. Sometimes they blasted their way through.

During the winter of 1867, they had to dig under the snow. This was just to reach a tunnel entrance. They chipped away at the rock. Crews worked 24 hours a day. Digging went on deep inside the mountain. Workers rarely saw the sun.

While one group of workers was digging the tunnel, another group crossed the mountain. Their job was to lay track on the east side. That's where the first track would come out of the tunnel. They had a big job to do. They took apart three locomotives and forty railroad cars.

They dragged those pieces on **sleighs** over the snowy mountain. There were tons of other material, too. Each iron rail weighed 600 pounds! Yet the men dragged plenty of supplies over the mountain. They had enough to lay 50 miles of track the next spring.

This is one of the huge tunnels that workers dug through solid rock in the Sierra Mountains.

Vo·cab·u·lar·y

sleighs (slayz)—vehicles on runners, like large sleds

[158]

Haste Made Waste—Also Great Wealth

Both companies raced to lay track. Soon they began to take shortcuts. The Central Pacific workers laid track around hills. Later, it cost millions of dollars to straighten out the curves.

During the winter of 1868, the Union Pacific workers hammered rails into ice. In the spring, the ice melted. Then large parts of track gave way. ⦿ ....

The men who headed up the companies became millionaires. They were called the "Big Four." Many people hated them. People didn't like the way the men treated their workers. For example, the leaders demanded that workers put in long hours. But often, the workers received very low pay. Sometimes they had to wait for weeks or longer for their money.

Strategy

Interact With Text by identifying how the text is organized.

My Thinking
Earlier in the selection, the text said Central Pacific crews were digging tunnels in the winter of 1867. Now it talks about the Union Pacific workers during the winter of 1868. So the text is still following time order.

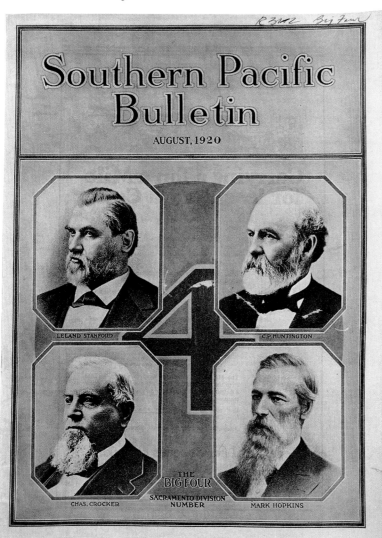

The "Big Four" were Leland Stanford, Colis P. Huntington, Charles Crocker, and Mark Hopkins.

Reaching the End

It was late spring in 1869. The workers from the two railroad companies could see each other. They were nearing Promontory Point, Utah. On May 10, 1869, the two sections of track met. This was thanks to the work of 20,000 men. The two locomotives faced each other. They nearly touched. Their trip to this spot had taken three years. Workers had laid over 1,175 miles of new track.

People had come to celebrate. A band played for the huge crowd. The boss of the Central Pacific tried to hammer in a golden spike. It was to connect the two sections of track. He missed! Then the boss of the Union Pacific tried. He also missed!

One of the workers finally slammed the spike into place. That spike completed the first cross-country railroad. This success would change our country forever. The new railroad was ready. It would help move people from coast to coast.

Strategy

Interact With Text by identifying how the text is organized.

My Thinking
The text is still telling the order of when things happened. Work on the railroad really got started in 1865. Over just a few years, an awful lot of work was done. Now I read that by 1869, the railroad across the country was finished. There had been some big mistakes, but the last spike was pounded in on May 10, 1869.

This scene is at Promontory Point, Utah, as the first transcontinental railroad is finished.

Setting a Record*

length of track	10 miles, 56 feet
number of ties	25,800
number of rails	3,520
number of spikes	28,160
number of bolts	14,080

Workers for the Union Pacific Railroad Company set this record in one day, on April 28, 1869.

Think About the Strategy

AFTER READING

Evaluate

by forming a judgment about whether the selection was objective or biased.

My Thinking

The strategy says to evaluate by forming a judgment about whether the selection was objective or biased. I know that objective text tells the truth without taking sides. So biased text must favor one side or the other in a situation. I think this selection was objective because it told the story in order of how it happened. It told about successes the workers and businessmen had. But it also told about problems they faced and that the businessmen were not always fair.

Graphic organizers help us organize information. An order chain organizes events in time order. It shows how one step follows another step. To get started, you ask, "What happened or was done first?" Then you need to figure out the other steps in order. Finally, you identify the last, or final step.

Order Chain

Topic – Bringing East and West Together
First Step – People saw the need for a railroad across the whole country. (1850s)
Next Step – President Lincoln signed the Railroad Act. (1862)
Next Step – Two railroad companies were formed. (1865)
Next Step – The two companies hired workers. (1866)
Next Step – The Union Pacific company laid tracks toward the west. (1866)
Next Step – The Central Pacific company laid tracks toward the east. (1866)
Next Step – Both companies overcame many problems and kept building. (1867–1868)
Next Step – Success—the two railroads met at Promontory Point, Utah. (1869)

I used my graphic organizer to write a summary of the article. Can you find the information in my summary that came from my order chain?

A Summary of
Bringing East and West Together

Have you ever ridden on a train? Long ago, there were no cars. People rode in trains instead. The trains were all in the East. They went no farther west than the Mississippi River. People wanted the trains to go across the whole country.

In 1862, President Abraham Lincoln decided to solve this problem. He signed the Railroad Act. This act paid two companies to build a railroad across the country. The Union Pacific Railroad Company started in Omaha, Nebraska. It laid railroad tracks toward the west. The Central Pacific Railroad Company started in Sacramento, California. It laid tracks toward the east.

Both companies faced many problems. They could not find enough workers. Blizzards made it very hard to lay track. Native Americans tried to stop the work. They did not want the railroad to end their way of life.

Finally, the two sets of tracks met. The place was Promontory Point, Utah. It was in May of 1869. Now trains could run across the whole nation. They would change our country forever.

Introduction
Here is my introduction. It tells what I will write about. The main idea is the topic of my order chain.

Body
I used information from each step in my order chain for the paragraphs in the body of my summary.

Conclusion
I summarized my paper by giving the final step in the building of the railroad.

Words Inside Words

Words in English sometimes contain smaller words or parts of words. The meaning of the **inside word** often tells you something about the meaning of the whole word. For instance, the word *personal* contains the word *person*. *Personal* means "private, or having to do with one *person* only."

Read this passage from the selection "Bringing East and West Together":

> *Both companies had a problem, though. They couldn't find enough men for the hard work. At that time, not many people lived in California. The Central Pacific Railroad took a chance. It hired some Chinese* **immigrants**.

The word *immigrant* contains the word *migrant*. It also contains most of the word *migrate*. *Migrant* and *migrate* can help you understand what *immigrant* means.

The word *migrate* means "to move from one country or region to another." The word *migrant* means "a person who moves around doing seasonal work."

Now look back at the passage above. The clues in the passage are *hired* and *Chinese*. When you put the meanings of *migrant* and *migrate* with the clues, you can understand the word *immigrant*. An **immigrant** is "a person who comes from one country to live permanently in another country."

> Read these sentences from the selection. Notice the underlined word or word part in each boldface word. Use your knowledge of the meaning of the inside word and the clues in the sentence to write a definition of the boldface word. Write your answers on a separate sheet of paper.
>
> 1. The trip was too long and **dangerous**.
> 2. The steam **locomotive** was invented in 1850.
> 3. This was because the **government** paid so well.
> 4. Nearly 80 **percent** of the Central Pacific workers were Chinese.
> 5. The men who headed up the companies became **millionaires**.

Readers' Theater

This Readers' Theater is about the railroad bosses' celebration after tracks of the Union Pacific and Central Pacific railroad companies were joined. Practice this script several times with two partners until you are ready to perform it for an audience.

Fluency TIP

Take turns reading the parts of the two bosses and the worker. Remember to read with expression, matching your tone of voice to the personality of each character.

The Railroad Bosses Celebrate at Promontory Point

Central Pacific Boss: Welcome, all! Thank you for coming out to join us on this very special day!

Union Pacific Boss: Today, May 10, 1869, is a day that will go down in history!

CP Boss: Indeed it will!

UP Boss: We have done an amazing thing. At least 1,175 miles of new track have been laid over the past three years.

CP Boss: What an amazing accomplishment!

UP Boss: Some 20,000 workers gave their blood, sweat, tears, and even lives to complete this railroad.

CP Boss: The whole country is thankful.

UP Boss: Now, for the first time, travelers may ride from coast to coast without interruption.

CP Boss: Imagine that! And to mark this momentous occasion, I will now hammer in a golden spike. This spike will officially complete the first cross-country railroad. Harrrrumph! Wow, this hammer is heavy! (Bang!) I got it! Oops, why is the spike rolling away?

UP Boss: Let me try. Um, this is hard.

Worker: Oh, brother!

UP Boss: Ouch! I missed the spike and hit my toe!

CP Boss: Can anyone here hammer in this spike?

Worker: Give me the hammer before you hurt anything else. (Bang!) There! Now it's done.

Think About
the
Strategies

BEFORE READING

Activate Prior Knowledge
by reading the introduction and/or summary to decide what I know about this topic.

 Write notes on your own paper to tell how you used this strategy.

DURING READING

Interact With Text
by identifying how the text is organized.

 When you come to a red button like this ⬤, write notes on your own paper to tell how you used this strategy.

The Orphan Trains

Introduction

In 1854, 46 **orphaned** children, ages 10 to 12, got on a boat in New York City. The boat took them down a river to a train. The train took them to another boat. Finally, a second train carried them to Dowagiac, Michigan. Within a week of arriving in the small town, all of these children had new homes.

The people who organized this first orphan train were thrilled with its success. They arranged for more orphan trains. By 1930, about 200,000 children had ridden the orphan trains. They had traveled from crowded cities on the East Coast to small towns in 47 states.

Vo•**cab**•u•lar•y

orphaned (or•fuhnd)— without parents

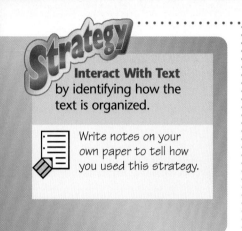

Strategy

Interact With Text
by identifying how the text is organized.

Write notes on your own paper to tell how you used this strategy.

Were the orphan trains a good thing? We can ask the orphans who rode them. Some of them are still alive today. Many tell about loving families. These people took them in. Most families treated their new family members well. The orphans grew up happy and cared for. Some even became famous. For example, one orphan was named John Brady. He became governor of the Alaska Territory. This was before Alaska became a state. A boy named Andre Burke also rode the orphan trains. When he grew up, he was elected governor of North Dakota.

Some were taken in by families who just wanted help with farm chores. Some weren't loved very much. But lots of them were loved. And they did very well.

Struggling on the Streets

Why were orphans sent away on trains? In the middle and late 1800s, thousands of children lived in large cities on the East Coast. Many of the children were homeless. But not all were orphans. Some had families that could not care for them. Others were living with families that **abused** them.

Many were children of parents who had come to the U.S. from other countries. Often, these people spoke little or no English. They were not prepared for the hard living conditions they found. It was especially hard when they were not able to find work. Without an income, they couldn't support their families. This forced many children out onto the streets. Others were turned over to orphanages or to other groups who tried to care for homeless or needy children.

Sometimes, a woman whose husband had died had to give up one or more of her children when she couldn't afford to keep them on her own. And babies born to girls or women who weren't married might end up in an orphanage.

Most of the children on the streets were cold in winter. And they were hungry all year round. They rarely went to school. They were almost never taken to a doctor when they got sick.

Life was hard on the streets. Some children sold flowers, matches, newspapers, or rags. Others sang on street

Vo•cab•u•lar•y

abused (uh•**byoozd**)—hurt or treated badly

corners or in bars, hoping for a few coins. The children needed the little bit of money they earned to survive. Others begged for or stole what they needed.

To protect themselves from danger and violence, they often got together in gangs. Many turned to crime. If they were caught, they were put in jail. At that time, there weren't any special jails for children. They were locked up with adult criminals.

A minister named Charles Loring Brace lived in New York City. He saw the children suffering and wanted to help. In 1853, he set up the Children's Aid Society. He knew the children needed, first of all, a safe place to live. But he did not want to crowd them into the **orphanages** in the city. And he really hated finding children in jail.

Strategy

Interact With Text by identifying how the text is organized.

Write notes on your own paper to tell how you used this strategy.

He knew there was much more room out West. At that time, "out West" meant the small farming towns at the far ends of the railroad tracks. These towns were in a region that we now call the Midwest. Brace thought that families out West would be glad to take the children.

Orphans traveling west

Vo•**cab**•u•lar•y

orphanages
(**or**•fuh•nij•ez)—places that care for orphans

Brace planned to use trains to carry the children to their new towns. When the children arrived, a **committee** of people from that town would help them find good homes. Brace's idea turned into the largest **migration** of children in U.S. history.

At first, these trains were not called "orphan trains." This moving of children to new homes in the West was called "placing out." The people in these placing-out groups thought that people out West would welcome the children.

New Homes for Orphans*

Arkansas	136†
Illinois	9,172
Indiana	3,955
Iowa	6,675
Michigan	5,326
Missouri	6,088
Nebraska	3,442
North Dakota	975
Ohio	7,272
South Dakota	43

*from a report by the Children's Aid Society, 1910
†numbers of children

As you can see in this chart, over time thousands of children were relocated to homes in many different states.

Riding the Trains

The trains usually left New York City on Tuesday. That way, they would arrive at different places over the weekend. The children rode the trains in groups. A group might be 3 children—or 300. They usually **ranged** in age from 1 month to 12 years. Many of the children came from orphanages. But some were given up by their families. Others came directly off the streets. Some children even asked to go on the trains.

The trips to the West took three to five days. Often the children were not told why they were going on the trip. Each child was given clothes to wear on the train. The children also received dress-up clothes. They would put these on just before they arrived at their new town.

Certain people were called placing agents. They rode with the children and took care of them. They gave the children Bibles. They sang to them so that they wouldn't be afraid. The agents would help "place" the children in new families. These agents packed sandwiches and other food for the trip. They also took along soap and wash-cloths. Sadly, there often was no room for toys or books. And the children often slept in their seats.

Waiting to Be Chosen

As the train neared a town, the children washed their faces. They changed their clothes. The girls wore new dresses. The boys wore white shirts, neckties, and suit coats. A thousand people might be waiting to see them. Not all of these people wanted to take a child. Many came just to watch the excitement.

The children got off the train. They were looked at and talked to so that everyone had time to begin to know them. Then the families made their choices. It was sad that sometimes brothers and sisters were chosen by different families. Children who were not chosen were put back on the train. They went on to the next town.

The placing agents tried to visit the children twice a year in their new homes. They wanted to see how they were doing. Some children were taken from families that **mistreated** them. They were given to another family.

Farming in the West was growing quickly, and many farmers needed new workers. Some of the older children became **indentured** workers. The families accepted them for the farming or housework they could do. After the time in the agreement passed, the child usually was nearly an adult. Then he or she was free to find a new life.

Many of the children met new problems when they grew up. For example, the placing-out groups had rules. The children were never supposed to try to find their real parents. Often they did not even have birth certificates.

Vo•cab•u•lar•y

mistreated (mis•**tree**•tid)— treated roughly or badly; abused

indentured (in•**den**•chuhrd)—bound by a signed contract to work for another person, usually for a certain length of time

Many people were happy to take a new child into their home.

A person has to have a birth certificate to get other legal papers. For example, without a birth certificate, a person has a lot of trouble getting a passport or a driver's license. Some of the orphans who grew up and went to fight in World War I had trouble getting back into the country. They didn't have passports! Also, children who were not officially adopted by their new families were not allowed to inherit anything when their parents died.

After they grew up, though, many orphans did go back East to try to find their families. Some succeeded, but most did not. Finding records of what had happened to the children was often very hard. Many of the orphanages no longer existed. Their records had either been lost or destroyed.

Over time, stories of the orphan trains became public. Former orphans were able to track down brothers and sisters they had been separated from. Orphans began to form groups to help one another find their histories. Many are finding information on the Internet. Many of the groups have begun to set up reunions. Orphan train survivors and their children can get together and compare stories. Little by little, the survivors and their families are putting the pieces of information together. They are building family histories.

Strategy

Interact With Text by identifying how the text is organized.

Write notes on your own paper to tell how you used this strategy.

Shaping the Nation

By 1930, new laws were helping protect orphans and other needy children. They were no longer sent away on trains. Most of the orphans from the trains grew up in their new homes. They were far from where they had been born. They had families of their own. Their children and grandchildren live throughout the Midwest and the Great Plains. In this way, the orphan trains helped shape our nation.

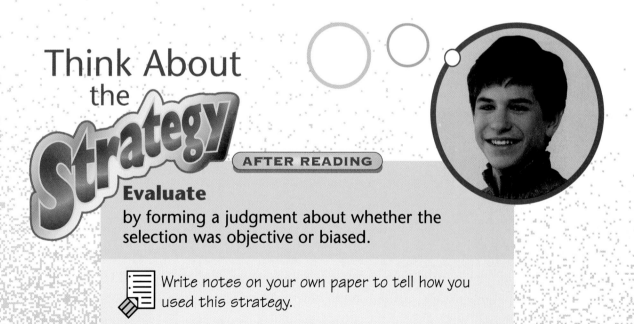

Think About the Strategy

AFTER READING

Evaluate

by forming a judgment about whether the selection was objective or biased.

Write notes on your own paper to tell how you used this strategy.

Vocabulary

Prefixes

A **prefix** is a word part that comes at the beginning of a word. Knowing the meaning of a prefix can help you understand the whole word.

As you read this passage from "The Orphan Trains," think about the meaning of the word with the prefix *mis-*.

> *The placing agents tried to visit the children twice a year in their new homes. They wanted to see how they were doing. Some children were taken from families that **mistreated** them. They were given to another family.*

To understand *mistreated,* break it up into its parts:

		Prefix		**Root**		**Suffix**
mistreated	=	*mis*	+	*treat*	+	*ed*

The first part of the word, *mis-*, is a prefix that means "bad or wrong." The root word *treat* means "to act in a particular way toward someone or something." The last part of the word, *-ed*, is an ending that tells you the action happened in the past. When you put the meanings of the word parts together, you know that *mistreated* means "acted roughly, cruelly, or badly toward someone or something."

On a separate sheet of paper, break up the following words into their prefix and root. Then use what you know about the word parts to write the definition for each word. If you need help, use a dictionary.

1. misuse
2. misbehave
3. misfortune
4. misplace
5. misunderstand
6. misread
7. misconduct
8. mistake
9. misdirect
10. mislead

Letter

Imagine that the following letter was written by an orphan named Ben while he was on a train. The letter is to his friend Johnny, back at the orphanage. Practice reading this letter aloud several times to a partner.

Fluency TIP

Remember to make your voice go up at the end of a question and to read the exclamations with excitement.

A Letter to Johnny From Ben

July 12, 1854

Dear Johnny,

I promised I'd write to you, and I always keep my promises! It was only eight days ago that we said good-bye, but it feels like years! I do miss you and the other boys. But I'll never miss life at the orphanage.

Perhaps you, too, will soon be aboard a train heading west! Here's what they won't tell you before you board: Once you get on the train, you'll never return to New York City. You see, the trains take us out to the far-off country. There, the farming folk can take their pick of orphans to adopt. Did you ever think your old friend Ben would wind up a farm boy? What an idea!

Yesterday the train stopped. The agents made us wash our faces and put on crisp shirts. They marched us off the train and through the center of a small town. Many people came and stared at us. One woman grabbed my wrist and asked me, "You know how to follow orders, boy?" Her teeth were brown, and her clothes were dirty. She scared me, so I freed my hand and shouted, "No!" After I made a ruckus, no one in that town wanted me. So now I'm back on the train, chugging along to the next small town. I do hope that there is a family out there who will want me—a family I will want to be with, too!

Yours truly,

Ben

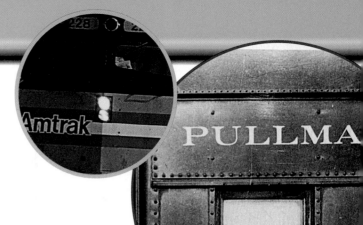

Think About
the
Strategies

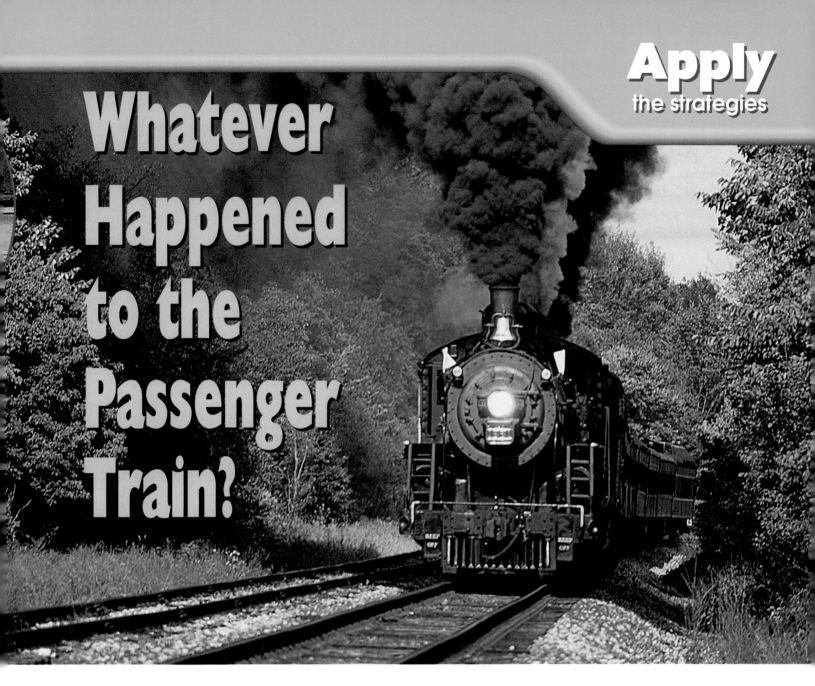

Whatever Happened to the Passenger Train?

Introduction

The 1900s began. More railroad tracks were being laid. Soon trains reached all over our country. They were a favorite way to travel.

By the late 1920s, 20,000 trains were running. People went on business trips. They made family visits. In many towns, trains stopped each day.

By 1970, though, things had changed. Only 450 passenger trains were still running in the whole United States. Many towns had no train service.

The number of people in the U.S. was growing quickly. Yet the number of miles people traveled by train dropped nearly 80 percent.

How did this happen? There is no one answer. But we can learn more about what happened. We can learn the history of trains.

Riding Through the 1930s and World War II

Trains played a main role during the Great Depression. This was in the 1930s. Millions of Americans were homeless. And they were hungry. They picked food out of trash cans. The often ate it even if it was spoiled. They slept under newspapers. They found shelter in cardboard boxes.

Many young men left home. That made one less mouth to feed. Many older men left home, too. Then their families could get help. They might get aid from the government.

A hobo riding the rails

By 1932, about a million people were roaming the nation. They were called **hoboes**. Mostly, they looked for work.

Many hoboes were women. They were as hungry as the men. But they couldn't dress like women. If they did, they were even less likely to find work.

[178]

Many hoboes **hitchhiked** on trains. They went from town to town. Then they moved on to the next state. They kept looking for work.

The Depression years kept train guards busy. Many worked at the Southern Pacific Railroad. They threw 683,000 hoboes off their trains.

The hoboes hid where they could on the trains. The best spot was in a luggage car or a boxcar. Some risked riding with the cattle!

There was a daring place to ride. It was on the very front of the train. But a little bounce could throw a rider off. In 1932, 1,886 hoboes slipped under train wheels and were killed.

Pullman cars encouraged people to take longer trips.

The trains were in trouble. They began to lose money during the 1930s. Few people could afford to buy a ticket.

Then World War II began. Trains were busy again. They were used for the armed forces. They moved almost all the war goods. They also moved nearly all the **troops** who were traveling.

At last the war ended. But the railroad companies were worried. They wanted people to keep riding the trains. So they made them smaller, faster, and nicer.

They added Pullmans. These are "sleeper-coaches." Then people could travel overnight. Some coaches had **domes**. Riders could sightsee as they rode.

By the late 1940s, trains were popular again. And they were making money.

But the trains had been worn out during the war. Now the railroads were unable to replace them. They could not get the supplies they needed. Worker **strikes** caused **delays**.

Vo·**cab**·u·lar·y

hitchhiked (**hich**•hykt)—traveled by getting free rides

troops—soldiers

domes (dohmz)—large windows in the roofs of some railroad passenger cars

strikes (stryks)—work stoppages by workers

delays (di•**layz**)—times when work can't continue

The companies should have built more than 4,000 new cars a year. In 1946, they made only 285 new coaches. The nation's trains were run-down. And they were not getting any better.

Facing New Problems

The railroads were going downhill. And people were taking to the air. Planes were no longer needed to fight the war. Now they carried passengers. And there was more bad news for the trains.

Detroit car builders began making millions of cars. In 1920, there were 8 million cars in the country. By 1930, there were 23 million. Some people running for office made wild offers. They promised a new car in every garage.

In 1940, drivers traveled 240 billion miles in their new cars. They went only 30 billion miles in trains. Our nation was just starting to make safe, good roads. And the new cars tended to break down. Cars were good for short trips. But people liked trains for longer journeys.

Then in 1956, the government took action. It urged states to build more and better roads. By this time, almost 90 percent of all travel in the country was by car. But the airlines continued to grow. More people were riding buses, too.

In 1967, the U.S. Post Office made a choice. It started to send first-class mail by plane. It had been using the train.

All these things helped cause the near-death of passenger trains.

Stepping In

The government wanted to save train service. In 1970, Congress set up the National Railroad Passenger Corporation. It aimed to run trains between big cities. This system of trains was first called Railpax. Now it is called Amtrak.

Amtrak bought the old trains. It rented track from railroad companies. Trains began running as Amtrak. But the average railroad car was 20 years old. And it was in poor shape.

Cars came from different railroads. Sometimes they could not link together. Poor tracks forced trains to run slowly. They often were late.

Still, by 1982, most of the old cars had been replaced. Amtrak also bought track and repaired it. Trains went between Boston, New York City, and Washington, D.C. They could travel up to 120 miles per hour.

There were 16.6 million riders in 1972. There were 20 million in 1997. By the end of the 1990s, things had changed. Amtrak had more than 400 locomotives. It ran 2,000 passenger cars. They traveled over 24,000 miles of track.

Some years Amtrak loses money. Then the government steps in. It makes up for the losses. The goal is to keep trains running in the United States.

Passenger trains made a way for Americans to travel long before the car and the plane. And they still play a major role, especially near big cities.

Amtrak's Busiest Train Stations, 2003*

Station	Number of Riders
1. New York, NY	4,261,741
2. Philadelphia, PA	1,796,583
3. Washington, DC	1,794,435
4. Chicago, IL	1,093,887
5. Newark, NJ	672,291
6. Los Angeles, CA	611,979
7. Trenton, NJ	495,593
8. Boston, MA	473,311
9. Princeton Jct., NJ	436,898
10. Sacramento, CA	431,891

*from Amtrak's Web site

This chart shows Amtrak's 10 busiest train stations in 2003.

Vocabulary

Common and Proper Nouns

A **common noun** is the general name of a person, place, or thing. A **proper noun** names a specific person, place, or thing. You can tell the difference between common nouns and proper nouns by looking for a capital letter at the beginning of a word. For example, if you read about the *White House* in Washington, D.C., you would know it is a specific place by the capital letters. However, there might also be a *white house* at the end of your street. Notice that *white* is an adjective, but it is part of the name of the proper noun. So it also starts with a capital letter.

In the selection "Whatever Happened to the Passenger Train?" you read about poverty during the *Great Depression.* That was a time in the U.S. from 1929 to 1939.One meaning of the word *depression* is "a time when businesses do badly and many people become poor." There have been other times of poverty that are called a depression. Only one, however, is referred to as "the Depression," with a capital D. With a capital D, *Depression* always refers to the Great Depression in the 1930s.

Here are some other proper nouns that can be confused with common nouns:

civil war: a war between different groups of people within the same country

Civil War: the U.S. war between the North and South from 1861 to 1865

president: the elected leader or chief executive of a republic; the head of a company, society, or organization

U.S. President: the current elected leader of the United States

Read these sentences from the selection. On a separate sheet of paper, write the nouns from each sentence. Then write whether each one is a common noun or a proper noun.

1. Trains played a main role during the Great Depression.
2. The Depression years kept train guards busy. Many worked at the Southern Pacific Railroad.
3. Then World War II began. Trains were busy again.
4. In 1967, the U.S. Post Office made a choice. It started to send first-class mail by plane.
5. The goal is to keep trains running in the United States.

Parody

A **parody** is a humorous imitation of another piece of writing. The following is a parody of a folksong about trains called "New River Train." Practice reading the lyrics, or words of the song, out loud with good rhythm, or beat. When you are ready, read it to an audience.

Song lyrics have strong rhythms. As you read this lyric, try to capture the rhythm of a moving train in your voice.

Parody of "New River Train"

Hitchin' on a passenger train,
Hitchin' on a passenger train,
I just keep on ridin' these lonesome rails
'Til I find some work again.

Hidin' from mean ol' train guards,
Hidin' from mean ol' train guards,
I gotta stow away in this luggage car
'Til the train stops in a yard.

Hitchin' on a passenger train,
Hitchin' on a passenger train,
I just keep on ridin' these lonesome rails
'Til I find some work again.

Tired of this hard hobo life,
Tired of this hard hobo life,
I'm missin' my home and family.
I'm even missin' my wife.

Hitchin' on a passenger train,
Hitchin' on a passenger train,
I just keep on ridin' these lonesome rails
'Til I find some work again.

Map

Rail Lines in the 1880s

This map shows the routes of the first railroads across the western part of our nation.

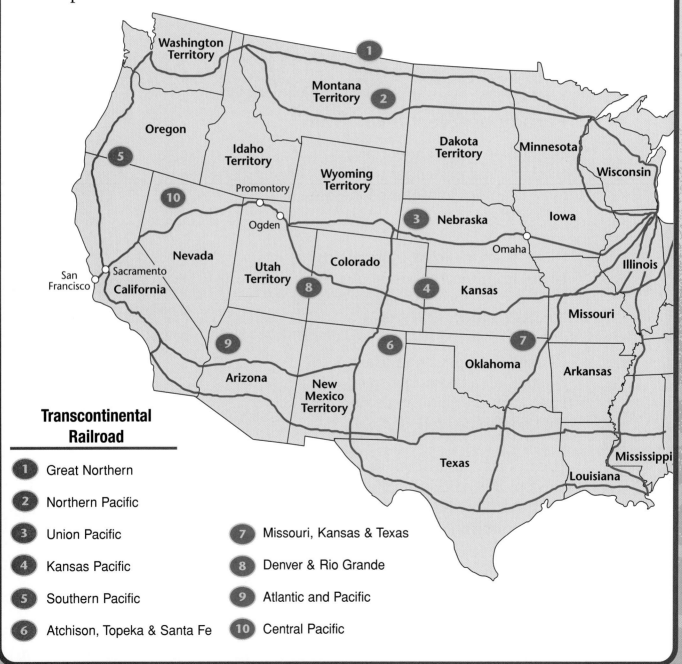

Transcontinental Railroad

1 Great Northern

2 Northern Pacific

3 Union Pacific

4 Kansas Pacific

5 Southern Pacific

6 Atchison, Topeka & Santa Fe

7 Missouri, Kansas & Texas

8 Denver & Rio Grande

9 Atlantic and Pacific

10 Central Pacific

Discussion Questions

Answer these questions with a partner or on a separate sheet of paper.

1. Which state did part of the first cross-country railroad pass through?
   a. Oregon
   b. Arizona
   c. Nevada
   d. Kansas

2. Did this part of the railroad pass through the state where you live?

3. Let's say a train leaves Omaha on this railroad. It is heading west. Where would it go after passing through Nebraska?

4. Promontory Point is almost on the border of which two places?
   a. Utah Territory and Idaho Territory
   b. Utah Territory and Colorado
   c. Nevada and Idaho Territory
   d. Wyoming Territory and Utah Territory

5. In which state did the workers have to lay track across the Sierra Mountains?
   a. Idaho
   b. Colorado
   c. Nebraska
   d. California

6. The two railroad companies began working at about the same time. One started in Sacramento. The other one started at Omaha. They should have met in the middle. Why did they meet closer to Sacramento than to Omaha?

7. Do you think this is still the only railroad in this part of the nation?
   a. Yes. This railroad track was so hard to lay that no one has tried to lay more.
   b. Yes. This railroad was so expensive that no one can afford to pay for another one.
   c. No. There are many more railroads now because many more people live in this part of the nation.
   d. No. There are many more railroads now because trains are our favorite way to travel.

8. The U.S. government paid to build a railroad from Omaha to Sacramento. Was that a good use of our money back then? Give reasons for your answer.

CONNECTING
to the Real World

Explore More

Trains in Other Lands
Interview a knowledgeable person or conduct research to learn the role trains play in travel in other places, such as Europe or Japan. Report the findings to the class.

Take a Trip
Consult a travel agent to get information on passenger train trips that are available today. Information should include areas of travel, prices, and accommodations for travelers. Use the collected information to prepare a bulletin board about travel on a modern passenger train.

Keep a Diary
Pretend you are an orphan on one of the orphan trains. Write a series of diary entries describing what you think, feel, and experience as you travel to your new home out West.

Sing a Song
Write and perform a song for the class that might have been sung as a "pep song" for workers on the transcontinental railroad project.

What It Was Like
Find out what traveling on a train in the late 1800s was like. Prepare an oral report, with pictures if possible, to present to the class.

Write an Essay
Imagine you are a hobo during the Great Depression. You want to travel to another town to look for work. In an essay, describe your plan. Tell what you do and what your experience is.

Related Books

Barter, James. *Building of the Transcontinental Railroad*. Lucent Books, Inc., 2002.

Dolan, Edward F. *The Transcontinental Railroad*. Benchmark Books, 2003.

Evans, Clark J. *The Central Pacific Railroad*. Children's Press, 2003.

Lassieur, Allison. *Passenger Trains*. Capstone Press, 2000.

Littlefield, Holly. *Children of the Orphan Trains*. Carolrhoda Books, Inc., 2001.

Macdonald, Fiona. *A 19th Century Railway Station*. Peter Bedrick Books, 1990.

O'Connor, Stephen. *Orphan Trains: The Story of Charles Loring Brace and the Children He Saved and Failed*. Houghton Mifflin Company, 2001.

Perl, Lila. *To the Golden Mountain: The Story of the Chinese Who Built the Transcontinental Railroad*. Benchmark Books, 2003.

Rach, Julie. *The Transcontinental Railroad*. Mason Crest Publishers, 2003.

Warren, Andrea. *We Rode the Orphan Trains*. Houghton Mifflin Company, 2001.

Interesting Web Sites

Check out these Web sites for more information about trains in United States history.

http://www.pbs.org/wgbh/amex/iron/index/html

http://www.hamilton.net/subscribers/hurd/reunion.htm

http://www.mindspring.com/~jjlanham/trcc1.htm

http://www.cprr.org/Museum/

http://www.sfmuseum.org/hist1/rail.html

http://www.rootsweb.com/~neadoptn/Orphan.htm

http://www.pbs.org/wgbh/amex/orphan/

http://www.suite101.com/article.cfm/history_for_children/18539

http://www.orphantrainriders.com/FAQ11.html

www.kancoll.org/articles/orphans/

http://www.geocities.com/railstudents/index.html

http://bushong.net/dawn/about/college/ids100/

BEFORE READING

Set a Purpose

by skimming the selection to decide what I want to know about this subject.

DURING READING

Clarify Understanding

by deciding whether the information I'm reading is fact or opinion.

AFTER READING

Respond

by forming my own opinion about what I've read.

LEARN
the strategies
in the selection
Alvin Ailey—Master of Dance
page 191

PRACTICE
the strategies
in the selection
Say to Yourself, "I AM an Artist!"
page 203

APPLY
the strategies
in the selection
Sculpture—It's the Whole World
page 211

Think About
the
Strategies

Set a Purpose

by skimming the selection to decide what I want to know about this subject.

My Thinking

The strategy says to skim the selection to decide what I want to know about this subject. When I skim something, I just look it over quickly. The title says that someone named Alvin Ailey is a master of dance. All the pictures and photos show people dancing or in dancelike poses.

As I skim the selection, I notice words such as *rehearsals, rhythm, dancers, studios,* and *ballet.* I like dancing, so I think I want to read on to find out who Alvin Ailey is and what he has to do with dancing.

DURING READING

Clarify Understanding

by deciding whether the information I'm reading is fact or opinion.

My Thinking

The strategy says to clarify understanding by deciding whether the information I'm reading is fact or opinion. I will stop and think about this strategy every time I come to a red button like this ●.

Alvin Ailey Master of Dance

Dance is not like other fine arts. It combines two great talents and skills. A good dancer must be creative. And he or she must be athletic. Good dancers are free in their thoughts and dreams. They are willing to imagine.

At the same time, they must be strong. They work hard in their workouts and **rehearsals**. They must practice. They often work for hours each day.

Vo•cab•u•lar•y

rehearsals (ri•**hur**•suhlz)— practice sessions before a performance

Vo·cab·u·lar·y

handbills (hand·bilz)—notices or advertisements

One American dancer mixed those two talents well. He grew famous around the world. He is Alvin Ailey.

Ailey was born in Roberts, Texas, on January 5, 1931. Every Sunday you could find him with his mother, Lula, at church. They went to the True Vine Baptist Church. This was in Navasota, Texas. Music was a big part of True Vine.

Alvin's mother sang in the choir. One of her favorite songs was "Rocka My Soul in the Bosom of Abraham." Alvin kept the beat of this music with him. He loved it for the rest of his life.

Soon Alvin was 12. He and his mother moved. They went to Los Angeles, California. Lula worked long hours, and Alvin had time on his hands. He spent that time looking around the city.

Often he walked past nightclubs. Some were along Central Avenue. He heard musicians there. They were rehearsing for their evening shows.

His favorite place was downtown. He liked the theater district. Alvin loved the lights. He loved the fuss around the theaters. Some of these theaters were the Biltmore, the Lincoln, and the Rosebud. He collected **handbills** from every show.

Alvin was outside the Biltmore one day. He saw another young man. The man was peeking in through the stage door. Alvin joined him. They watched. And they loved what they saw.

On stage, the Katherine Dunham Dancers were dancing. They would swirl, twirl, and lunge. They moved in ways Alvin had never seen. The music had a beat that Alvin had never heard.

Alvin was hooked. He went home that night. He told his mother about what he had seen and heard. He wanted more. He wanted to dance!

In 1949, not many dance studios took black students. But the Lester Horton School did. It welcomed anyone who was serious about dancing. Alvin was clearly serious.

At 18, he began studying with Horton. He went to the studio almost every day. Often, he danced all day. Sore muscles and sweat dripping down his face were common. That did not stop Alvin. He wanted to learn as much as he could.

Strategy

Clarify Understanding by deciding whether the information I'm reading is fact or opinion.

My Thinking
Near the beginning of this selection, the writer says Alvin was born in 1931, so in 1949 he would have been 18. And that's what the selection says, so that part is fact. The other parts, about how he worked so hard, making up his own stuff, and other dancers wanting to copy him could be opinion. But he did end up famous, so maybe that information is fact, too.

After a while, he began making up his own steps and movements. He seemed to hear and move to his own **rhythms**. Other dancers saw Alvin's work. They tried to copy what he was doing.

In 1950, Alvin joined Mr. Horton's dance company. He went with other dancers to perform. They danced for audiences outside the studio.

In 1953, Lester Horton had a heart attack and died. Alvin did not want the dance company to go out of business. So he took over. He became director and **choreographer**. A choreographer is a person who makes up the dances and lines up all the steps and movements.

In 1954, Alvin was invited to New York. His friend Carmen de Lavallade [day lah•val•**yah**•day] was asked, too. They went to dance in a Broadway show. It was *House of Flowers*. Alvin stayed in New York after the show. He danced in many ballets and more musicals.

Vo•cab•u•lar•y

rhythms (**rith**•uhmz)—beats

choreographer (kor•ee•**ahg**•ruh•fur)— a person trained in the art of creating and arranging the movements in dances

Alvin met and studied with important dancers. Some of them were Martha Graham, Doris Humphrey, and Charles Weidman. He longed to learn more. Through it all, he kept performing. And he kept on making up new dances.

In 1958, Alvin hired eight black dancers. He **founded** his own company. It was the Alvin Ailey American Dance Theater. He wanted to build a group that would join two worlds. He mixed modern dance with the music and culture of African Americans.

Alvin was very careful about the dancers he chose. He wanted dancers who were strong in body. And they were strong in **character**. He wanted people who were daring. They would not be afraid to try new things. They would work hard. He wanted every dancer to add something special to the group.

Alvin's way turned out to be the right one. The group gave its first show at the 92nd Street Y. This is in New York City. They performed *Blues Suite*. It was a series of dances set to blues music. The show was a huge success. Suddenly, Alvin's name was in all the newspapers.

In 1960, Alvin made up his most famous dance, *Revelations* [rev•uh•**lay**•shuhnz]. It was an American modern dance. He based it on the African American music of his childhood. His dances showed how people are often afraid. But they are also happy.

In *Revelations,* it seemed that all the years of Alvin's work and study came together.

It was an awesome show!

A group of dancers from the Alvin Ailey American Dance Theater

Vo•cab•u•lar•y

founded (**fown**•did)—started

character (**kar**•uhk•tuhr)— overall moral strength

Alvin Ailey in a dance pose

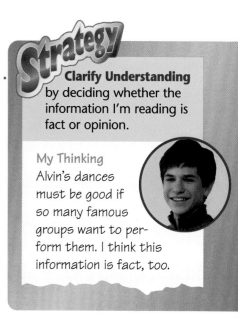

Strategy

Clarify Understanding by deciding whether the information I'm reading is fact or opinion.

My Thinking
Alvin's dances must be good if so many famous groups want to perform them. I think this information is fact, too.

Through the years, Alvin did dances by other choreographers as well as his own dances. He also began to include white dancers in his group.

In 1964, the company went on its first tour in Europe. They were a hit every place they danced. One of their shows was in Hamburg, Germany. At the end of the show, the audience stood. They clapped for more than 20 minutes!

Throughout his lifetime, Alvin worked hard. He created 79 ballets. Major dance groups around the world have performed many of them. Some of these are the American Ballet Theatre, Joffrey Ballet, Dance Theatre of Harlem, and Paris Opera Ballet.

Some of Alvin Ailey's Best-Known Dances

Performance Title	Year First Performed
Blues Suite	1958
Creation of the World	1961
Roots of the Blues	1961
Revelations	1960
Hermit Songs	1962
Cry	1971
Hidden Rites	1973
Night Creature	1975
Memoria	1979
The River	1981
At the Edge of the Precipice	1983

These are only a few of the dozens of dance performances Alvin created during his career.

"I Been Buked [byookt]" from *Revelations,* 1960

Photograph © Jack Mitchell

Alvin died on December 1, 1989. A great dancer and choreographer was gone. But his dances live on. They live in dancers around the world. The Alvin Ailey American Dance Theater continues his ideas of modern dance.

Anna Kisselgoff of *The New York Times* wrote, "You didn't need to have known Ailey personally to have been touched by his **humanity,** enthusiasm, and **exuberance** and his ideas for brotherhood."

Vo·cab·u·lar·y

humanity
(hyoo•**man**•i•tee)—
the quality of being human

exuberance
(ig•**zoo**•buhr•uhns)—
excitement or youthfulness

Think About the Strategy

AFTER READING

Respond
by forming my own opinion about what I've read.

My Thinking
The strategy says that I should respond by forming my own opinion about what I've read. Well, I don't know a lot about dancing, but this article gave a lot of information about Alvin and his life as a dancer. I liked the way the writer gave descriptions of how hard Alvin worked and about his success when audiences gave his dances standing ovations. I think Alvin would have been an interesting person to meet.

Graphic organizers help us organize information. A time line is a graph that shows events happening in order of time. Time lines show which event happened first, which came (in order) next, and which happened last.

Time Line
Alvin Ailey—Master of Dance

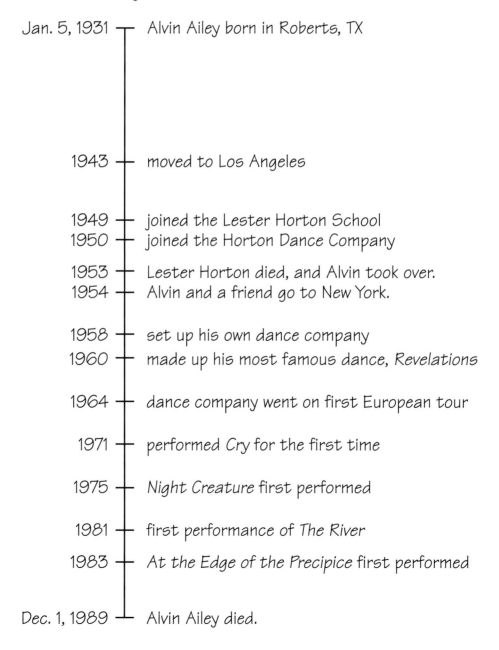

Jan. 5, 1931	Alvin Ailey born in Roberts, TX
1943	moved to Los Angeles
1949	joined the Lester Horton School
1950	joined the Horton Dance Company
1953	Lester Horton died, and Alvin took over.
1954	Alvin and a friend go to New York.
1958	set up his own dance company
1960	made up his most famous dance, *Revelations*
1964	dance company went on first European tour
1971	performed *Cry* for the first time
1975	*Night Creature* first performed
1981	first performance of *The River*
1983	*At the Edge of the Precipice* first performed
Dec. 1, 1989	Alvin Ailey died.

I used my graphic organizer to write a summary of the article. Can you find the information in my summary that came from my time line?

A Summary of
Alvin Ailey—Master of Dance

Alvin Ailey died when he was only 58. He had a short life. Still, he was a master who changed the art of dancing.

Alvin was born on January 5, 1931. He and his mother lived in Texas. In 1943, they moved to Los Angeles. Alvin was 12. He saw dancers for the first time. He wanted to dance, too. In 1949, Alvin began dancing. He went to the Lester Horton School. He was a good student. The next year, Alvin joined the Horton Dance Company. In 1953, Mr. Horton died. Alvin took over his dance company.

In 1954, Alvin and a friend went to New York. Alvin really liked Broadway. He stayed in New York. In 1958, he started his own dance company. He liked modern dance. He also liked African American music. He used both of them.

In 1960, Alvin made up a new dance. He called it *Revelations*. His dance became famous. Four years later, his dancers toured in Europe. People loved Alvin's dances. Since then, many groups have performed them.

Alvin died on December 1, 1989. He is gone. Still, his dances will *go on and on*.

Introduction
Here is my introduction. It tells what I will write about. The main idea is the title of my time line.

Body
I used information from my time line for the paragraphs in my body copy. The time line helped me write about Ailey in time order.

Conclusion
I summarized my paper by recalling the last part of my time line.

Time Order Words

There are certain words that tell you the order of events or time between events in a story. Words such as *first, next,* and *then* are **time order words**. Time order words signal you to think about the sequence of events when you are reading.

The article "Alvin Ailey—Master of Dance" is about the life of Alvin Ailey. The article starts when he was born and ends at his death. The author tells you about events in his life in the order they happened. Usually, the writer told you the order of events by giving the date or the year for each one. Look at this sentence from the article:

In 1949, not many dance studios took black students.

The writer also used time order words to tell you when events happened. Read the following sentence that appears in the selection three paragraphs later.

After a while, he began making up his own steps and moments.

Even though the writer does not tell you the exact year, the time order word *after* tells you that Alvin Ailey began making up his own steps some time later than 1949.

The sentences below name events in Alvin Ailey's life. On a separate sheet of paper, use the sentences to write a paragraph about Alvin Ailey. Choose some of the time order words below to use instead of the dates in the sentences to show the proper order of the events.

first	second	lastly	then
next	after	soon	later

1. In 1943, Alvin Ailey and his mother moved to Los Angeles, California.
2. In 1949, Alvin Ailey joined the Lester Horton School.
3. In 1953, Alvin Ailey became the director and choreographer of the Lester Horton School.
4. In 1954, Alvin Ailey was invited to dance in a Broadway show in New York City.
5. In 1964, Alvin Ailey's Dance Company toured Europe.

Poetry

A **cinquain** is a kind of poem that has five lines. The first line names the subject. The second line describes it. The third line lists action words about the subject. The fourth line is a phrase describing a feeling about the subject. The last line is a word that means almost the same thing as the first word. Practice reading these cinquains several times until you are ready to read them smoothly to an audience.

Practice pausing at different places in each poem until you find the most comfortable and effective way to read each line. Think about why you choose to pause in that place.

Three Dance Cinquains

Cinquain 1
dance
grace, style
spinning, leaping, bending
makes me feel free
movement

Cinquain 2
beat
pulse, sound
thumping, tapping, pounding
keeps time for me
rhythm

Cinquain 3
hip-hop
urban, music
rhyming, sliding, beating
born from rock and soul
culture

Think About
the
Strategies

BEFORE READING

Set a Purpose

by skimming the selection to decide what I want to know about this subject.

 Write notes on your own paper to tell how you used this strategy.

DURING READING

Clarify Understanding

by deciding whether the information I'm reading is fact or opinion.

 When you come to a red button like this ⬤, write notes on your own paper to tell how you used this strategy.

Say to Yourself, "I AM an Artist!"

As a little girl, Sheila Hamanaka [hah•muh•**nah**•kah] loved horses. She lived in New York City. She couldn't keep a horse there. Her family didn't have a lot of money. They couldn't pay for riding lessons. The only horses Sheila got to see were police horses.

Then one day she found a book. The book had pictures of fine horses inside. Sheila wanted to draw horses. Her art could be a way of having horses close to her.

First Sheila tried to **trace** around pictures in the book. It wasn't as easy as she thought. Her pencil seemed to have a mind of its own. Her lines went all over the place. Drawing was much harder than it looked!

Vo•cab•u•lar•y

trace (trays)—to copy by putting a piece of thin paper over a picture and drawing the outline of the picture

Strategy

Clarify Understanding by deciding whether the information I'm reading is fact or opinion.

Write notes on your own paper to tell how you used this strategy.

Sheila did not give up, though. She kept tracing other people's drawings. She learned to control the pencil. Then she started making her own drawings. Her favorite things were still horses.

People started saying good things about her work. They said things like "You're going to be an artist!"

Sheila took the words to heart. Her talent and practice helped her get good grades in school. She did really well when she could use art. She might make a poster, a **diorama,** or an illustrated report.

In high school, Sheila took lots of art courses. She studied the great artists from Europe. Later she studied Japanese, Asian, and Pacific art. She liked African and Latin American art, too. She wanted to learn as much as she could. She liked different styles and **mediums**.

This is the cover of the first book Sheila illustrated. She tried to include a variety of children in the drawing.

Vo·cab·u·lar·y

diorama (dy•uh•**ram**•uh)— a scene in which three-dimensional figures are displayed in a small setting

mediums (**mee**•dee•uhmz)—the materials used by artists

Sheila met a children's book **editor** in an exercise class. The editor helped her meet an art director. Sheila took some of her drawings and paintings for the director to see. Her first book contract came from that meeting. The art director liked Sheila's drawings of children. She was asked to illustrate a book called *Class Clown*.

Since then, Sheila has done many books. Some of them are *Screen of Frogs, Heart of the Wood, A Visit to Amy-Claire,* and *All the Colors of the Earth. The Journey* is a book Sheila both wrote and illustrated. It is based on a **mural**. She painted it about the Japanese in America.

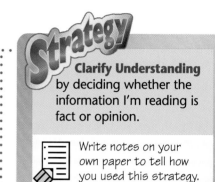

Strategy

Clarify Understanding by deciding whether the information I'm reading is fact or opinion.

Write notes on your own paper to tell how you used this strategy.

She still enjoys drawing horses. And she draws other animals and people. She uses them as models for characters in the books she illustrates.

Sheila remembers how she felt as a child. She was sad when she could not find books with Asian American characters. She doesn't want kids today to feel that sadness. So she draws all kinds of people. She makes girls and boys of all ages, colors, shapes, and sizes.

Sheila gets ideas for her paintings from many things. She remembers things from when she was growing up. She sees things out of her windows. She draws about her life. Sometimes a song, a magazine picture, or a good book will give her an idea. She also likes to talk to people. She tries to find out about their lives. Their stories give her more ideas.

As an artist, Sheila likes to **experiment** when she's painting. Mostly she paints in oils on canvas. She may use acrylic paints. She even uses colored pencils. She also likes to try things besides painting.

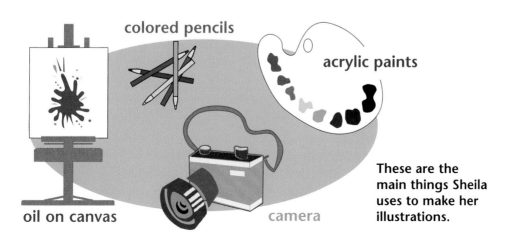

colored pencils

acrylic paints

oil on canvas

camera

These are the main things Sheila uses to make her illustrations.

Vo•**cab**•u•lar•y

editor (**ed**•i•tuhr)—someone who prepares written materials for publication

mural (**myur**•uhl)—a work of art painted on a wall

experiment (ik•**sper**•uh•muhnt)—to try new or different things

One time she used a camera. She took pictures for her book *In Search of the Spirit: The Living National Treasures of Japan*. She says someday she would like to try three-dimensional art, comics, and **animation**.

Strategy

Clarify Understanding by deciding whether the information I'm reading is fact or opinion.

Write notes on your own paper to tell how you used this strategy.

Moriguchi Kako is a designer of hand-painted kimonos and a "living national treasure of Japan."

These are two of the photos Sheila took for her book.

This kimono, titled "Colored Blossom," is one of Moriguchi Kako's designs.

Vo•cab•u•lar•y

animation
(an•uh•**may**•shuhn)—moving drawings, cartoons

Sheila believes her best tools are her eyes. She says, "Artists have different strengths. Some use colors well. Others put a lot of life and energy into their work. I thought that I would learn by looking. If I looked at the colors in the real world, in nature, my colors would look right, too. To draw realistic people or animals, it's important to study anatomy."

Sheila has won many awards for her work. She won the Jane Addams Peace Award and the American Book Award. She has gotten awards from Best Books for Young Adults and Best Books of the Year.

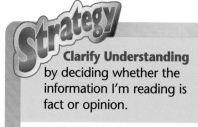

Strategy

Clarify Understanding by deciding whether the information I'm reading is fact or opinion.

Write notes on your own paper to tell how you used this strategy.

What do you think Sheila tells young artists? Well, she remembers her great love of horses. She remembers how she practiced. She worked for hours, days, and years to learn how to draw them.

"Pick something you love," she says, "—cars, people, flowers, dinosaurs—and keep drawing it. If no one tells you, 'You're going to be an artist,' then say it to yourself. Better yet, say, 'I **am** an artist.'"

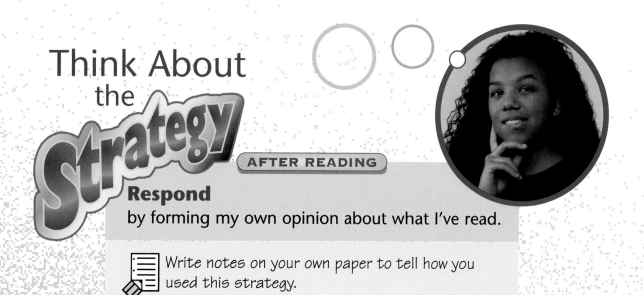

Think About the Strategy

AFTER READING

Respond by forming my own opinion about what I've read.

Write notes on your own paper to tell how you used this strategy.

Multiple Meanings

Many words have more than one meaning. You can find the correct meaning when you look at how the word is used in the sentence.

Read this passage from the selection "Say to Yourself, 'I AM an Artist!'" about Sheila Hamanaka:

She liked African and Latin American art, too. She wanted to learn as much as she could. She liked different styles and **mediums**.

Here is a list of some of the meanings of the word *medium*:

- middle or average
- the materials used by artists to express their ideas
- something on which information can be stored
- something used to communicate an idea to a lot of people
- something that carries or spreads something else

To find the correct meaning of the word *medium*, look for context clues in the excerpt. The excerpt is about art. Therefore the meaning of *mediums* is "the materials used by artists." Some examples of artists' *mediums* are paints, watercolors, and pencils.

Read the sentences below. Identify which meaning of the word *medium* from the above list is being used in each sentence. Write the words and your answers on a separate sheet of paper.

1. Air, insects, and some birds are **mediums** for pollen.
2. One **medium** of advertising is television commercials.
3. I bought a **medium** T-shirt at the clothing sale.
4. What **mediums** did the artist use in that collage?
5. A floppy disk is a good **medium** for collecting all of my journal entries.

Readers' Theater

The following script has four parts. It is about a class getting ready to paint a mural together. Practice reading this script in groups of four. Remember to read your character's words the way he or she might speak. When you are ready, perform the script for the class.

Fluency **TIP**

> Read this script to yourself a couple of times. Think about what the characters are like. Then, when you continue practicing the script, try to bring the personalities of the characters to life with your voice.

Mr. Brock: Does anyone have any ideas for our class mural?

Larry: Since it's almost Arbor Day, why don't we paint trees?

Mr. Brock: That's a fine idea, Larry! How do the rest of you feel about painting different kinds of trees?

Tenisha: It'll be fun! I know what a willow tree looks like. There's one at my grandma's house. I'm sure I could draw one if I practice.

Mr. Brock: That's a good start, Tenisha. Could you also look for pictures of other types of trees for the mural?

Maria: I like to paint flowers. Can we paint beautiful flowers around the base of the trees? It will look like a fantasy garden!

Mr. Brock: That sounds like a great addition. Let's break into groups and begin working. One group can research trees and practice drawing them. Another group can plan the kinds of flowers to be painted. A third group can begin to paint the background. Is there anything we're forgetting?

Tenisha: We forgot about art supplies. We need paints and brushes.

Larry: I'll go down to the art room and get the supplies. Then I'll start working on the background. We could use sponges to paint the sky and clouds.

Tenisha: I'll look in the encyclopedia for types of trees. Then I can use tracing paper and pencils to practice drawing them.

Maria: And I will research different kinds of flowers. There will be flowers of every color in the rainbow!

Mr. Brock: Great planning, everybody. Let's get started!

Think About the Strategies

BEFORE READING

Set a Purpose

by skimming the selection to decide what I want to know about this subject.

DURING READING

Clarify Understanding

by deciding whether the information I'm reading is fact or opinion.

AFTER READING

Respond

by forming my own opinion about what I've read.

 Use your own paper to jot notes to apply these Before, During, and After Reading Strategies. In this selection, you will choose when to stop, think, and respond.

Sculpture—It's the Whole World

Louise with some of her sculptures

Introduction

Louise Nevelson Plaza was a small park near Wall Street. It was the first public area in New York City that was named after an artist. Nevelson, a great American **sculptor,** made the seven giant sculptures displayed there.

Sadly, the park was lost on September 11, 2001. That's when terrorists flew two planes into the World Trade Center. The Center and the area around it were destroyed. But Louise Nevelson and the rest of her art are known all around the world.

Her Early Life

Louise Nevelson was born on September 23, 1899, in Kiev [kee•**ef**], Ukraine [yoo•**krayn**]. Her parents were Mina Sadie and Isaac Berliawsky [bair•**low**•skee].

Vo•cab•u•lar•y

sculptor (**skulp**•tuhr)—an artist who produces work by carving, molding, or welding

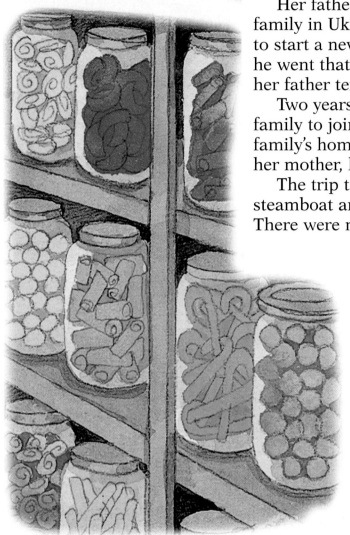

Her father was a lumber merchant. In 1902, he left his family in Ukraine. He moved to the United States. He left to start a new life for his family. Louise was so sad when he went that she did not talk for six months. She missed her father terribly.

Two years later, he had sent enough money for the family to join him in America. Louise's mother sold the family's home in Ukraine. Then they were off—Louise, her mother, her older brother, and her younger sister.

The trip took several months. They traveled by steamboat and train. They even used a horse cart. There were many stops along the way. Louise never forgot one of those stops. It was in Liverpool, England.

Louise's mother took her children into a candy store. They had never before seen anything like it. Stacks of shelves were everywhere. They were all filled with jars of sparkling hard candies. Louise was **fascinated**.

A New Home

Louise's family finally made it to Rockland, Maine. That's where they would live. Louise's father owned a lumberyard. He worked as a builder. And he was successful. The family had a lovely home.

Louise and her family were Jewish. Louise spoke only **Yiddish** and Russian. She did not understand English. She did not understand American people and **customs**. School was very difficult for her. And she had few friends.

There was one safe place in her school. Louise felt at home there. It was the art room. In the art room, Louise felt warm and comfortable. She loved what she did there. She decided to be an artist.

At home, Louise created and lived in her own **fantasy** world. She loved to paint. She made costumes and put on plays. Piano and art lessons took the place of friendships. From the time she was six, Louise gathered wood scraps from her father's lumberyard. She used them in her projects.

Vo•cab•u•lar•y

fascinated (**fas**•uh•nay•tuhd)—totally impressed

Yiddish (**yid**•ish)—a German language usually written in Hebrew characters and spoken by Jewish people from eastern Europe

customs (**kus**•tuhmz)—things that people have done for a long time

fantasy (**fan**•tuh•see)— make-believe

Moving On

In 1920, Louise married Charles Nevelson. They moved to New York City. In 1922, she gave birth to her only child, Myron.

But the life of a wife and mother was not the right one for her. She wanted to study art around the world. She wanted to work. She wanted to create.

In 1931, Louise left her husband. She took Myron to live with her parents in Maine. Then she went to Germany. She became a student of the great artist, Hans Hofmann [hahnz **hof**•muhn]. Louise also worked as an assistant to another great artist, Diego [dee•**ay**•goh] Rivera [ri•**vair**•uh].

Then the Nazis closed down the art school in Germany. Louise returned to the United States. For a while Louise taught at an art school. She worked on the Lower East Side of New York City. She was busy as a teacher. But she continued her own work.

The Artist at Work

The picture of the English candy store never left her. She could still see the stacks of shelves. She remembered the bright-colored candy.

She was still picking up pieces of wood. She hadn't lost her talent for finding creative uses for them. She spent hours building boxes. She filled them with things she found on the streets of Manhattan. She used wine crates, chair legs, rolling pins, and duck **decoys**. She said, "Wood picked up on the street can be gold."

In 1941, Louise had her first **exhibition** in New York. But her work was too different. No one would buy it. Louise often lived without enough money to buy food or pay the rent. But she did not give up. Her love of art kept her going.

The World Catches Up

Eighteen years later, Louise got a good surprise. She was invited to show her work. It would be at the Museum of Modern Art in New York City. She made a special sculpture for the show.

It was a collection of filled shelves and boxes. It took up an entire room. She had painted it all white. She called it *Dawn's Wedding Feast*. No other sculptor had ever done anything like it. Now people thought it was sensational. They had finally caught up with Louise.

Louise became famous for her work. She kept collecting bits and pieces of things. She made whole walls of box sculptures. She painted them black or white or gold. She called them "environments." "It's not only sculpture," she said. "It is a whole world."

An art **critic** once said Louise is a "cross between Catherine the Great and a bag lady."

Vo·cab·u·lar·y

decoys (dee•koyz)—artificial birds that hunters use to attract live birds

exhibition (ek•suh•**bish**•uhn)—a large, public showing or display

critic (**krit**•ik)—someone who makes judgments about or evaluates something, such as art

In her later years, Louise added plastic and aluminum to her art. She was hired for several public art projects. Her sculptures came to stand in the world's great museums.

She died in 1988. Just before then, she finished a black steel sculpture. It was for the National Institutes of Health in Bethesda [buh•**thez**•duh], Maryland. It is 35 feet high.

Louise Nevelson would not take "no" for an answer. She was not afraid of new ideas and new ways of doing things. She made her art the way she wanted to, not the way others thought it should be. She is an example of the power of creativity and courage.

Louise's sculpture at the National Institutes of Health

Sculptures and Works by Louise Nevelson		
Museum or Park	**Location**	**Title of Work**
National Museum of Women in the Arts	Washington, D.C.	*White Column* (from *Dawn's Wedding Feast*), 1959
National Gallery of Art	Washington, D.C.	Untitled work, 1963
Museum of Fine Arts, Boston	Boston, MA	*Mirror-Shadow VIII*, 1985
Guggenheim Museum	New York, NY	*Luminous Zag: Night*, 1971 *White Vertical Tower*, 1972
Meijer Sculpture Park	Grand Rapids, MI	*Atmosphere and Environment XI*, 1969
MIT Campus	Cambridge, MA	*Transparent Horizon*, 1975
Baltimore Museum of Art, Sculpture Garden	Baltimore, MD	*Seventh Decade Forest*, 1971–1976
Wells Fargo Center	Los Angeles, CA	*Night Sail*, 1985
Madison Plaza	Chicago, IL	*Dawn Shadows*, 1983
Albright-Knox Art Gallery	Buffalo, NY	Several works
The Tate Gallery	London, England	Several works
Hirshhorn Museum and Sculpture Garden	Washington, D.C.	Several works
Musee D'Art Moderne de la Ville de Paris	Paris, France	Several works

Nevelson's work is all over the world. This chart shows the locations of some of her pieces.

The Suffix *-tion*

A **suffix** is a word part that is added to the end of a word. Sometimes the meaning of the suffix can give a clue to the meaning of the word. Words with the suffix *-tion* are always nouns. The suffix *-tion* means "the state of, the act of, or the result of."

Look at this sentence from "Sculpture—It's the Whole World."

> *In 1941, Louise had her first **exhibition** in New York.*

To find the meaning of the word *exhibition,* break the word into the verb and suffix:

<u>verb</u>		<u>suffix</u>		<u>noun</u>
exhibit	+	*-tion*	=	*exhibition*

To *exhibit* means "to show publicly." The meaning of the verb *exhibit* plus the meaning of the suffix *-tion* suggests *exhibition* means "the act of publicly showing artwork." More precisely, it means "a large public showing or display."

Here are some other words with the suffix *-tion.*

relax(a) + tion = *relaxation: the state of being relaxed*
create + tion = *creation: the result of creating*
pollute + tion = *pollution: the result of polluting*

Read the following sentences. Each boldface word can be broken into a verb and the suffix *-tion*. Write the verb on a separate sheet of paper. Then think about what the verb and the suffix mean together. Write the meaning of the *-tion* word.

1. Artists use their **imagination** to think of new work.
2. It takes a lot of **determination** and hard work to be a successful artist.
3. The exhibition took five days of **preparation** to complete.
4. Some artists continue their **education** at an art school.
5. I felt the **sensation** that the sculpture was rough when I touched it.

Letter

Rosie and her grandmother went to a sculpture garden. After Rosie returned from a school field trip to an art museum, she wanted to tell her grandmother all about it. The following is a letter that Rosie might have written to her grandmother. Read the letter several times to yourself. Try to imagine how Rosie felt as you read the letter aloud to a partner.

> Many of the sentences in Rosie's letter are long. Place short pauses at the end of commas and at the end of phrases that are not marked by commas. These pauses will help the listener understand.

A Letter to Grandma

Dear Grandma,

I always love our walks to the sculpture garden when I come to visit you. You showed me how amazing sculpture can be, especially if the sculptor is Louise Nevelson!

Today, I finally saw one of Louise's famous "environments." My class went on a trip to the art museum. We saw lots of interesting and colorful paintings and sculptures. Suddenly, we entered a room that was completely white. One wall was covered with shelves from floor to ceiling. On those shelves were all kinds of wooden objects. But you really had to look closely to see what the objects were, because everything was white!

Louise's sculpture reminded me of a snowy day. On days like that, the world looks like it's covered by a white blanket. I wonder why Louise wanted to hide the colors of the objects she uses. Maybe it's because you start to appreciate colors even more when they are taken away. When we left the white room, the colorful pieces of the other artists looked even brighter!

I can't wait to go back to the museum to see the sculptures again. Maybe next time you and I can go together!

Love always,
Rosie

Schedule

A Schedule of Performances

The Alvin Ailey American Dance Theater performs many times a year. Look over this schedule for January 2004. Then answer the questions on the following page.

Ailey Performance Schedule

Dates	Cities	Locations
January 11	Chattanooga, TN	University of Tennessee
January 13	Newberry, SC	Newberry Opera House
January 14	Orangeburg, SC	Claflin University
January 15–16	Hilton Head, SC	Arts Center of Coastal Carolina
January 18	Brunswick, GA	Ritz Theatre
January 19	Augusta, GA	Imperial Theatre
January 21	Columbus, GA	Bill Heard Theatre
January 22	Milledgeville, GA	Russell Auditorium
January 23	Madison, GA	Madison-Morgan Cultural Center
January 25	Davidson, NC	Davidson College
January 26	Durham, NC	Duke University
January 27	Winston-Salem, NC	Kenneth R. Williams Auditorium
January 28	Knoxville, TN	University of Tennessee
January 30	Memphis, TN	Cannon Center for the Performing Arts

Discussion Questions

Answer these questions with a partner or on a separate sheet of paper.

1. Where did the dancers perform on January 25?

2. Where did the dancers go after they performed at the Newberry Opera House?

3. How often did the dancers perform in January of 2004?

4. In which state were most of the January performances?
   a. Tennessee
   b. South Carolina
   c. North Carolina
   d. Georgia

5. In which part of the United States were most of these performances?
   a. Northeast
   b. Southeast
   c. Northwest
   d. Southwest

6. Why do you think the dancers performed in South Carolina, then Georgia, then North Carolina?
   a. No one wanted to see them perform in other states.
   b. The dancers lived in these states.
   c. It was too cold to dance in other states in January.
   d. These states are close together, so the dancers had to travel less.

7. Look over this schedule. How popular is the Alvin Ailey Dance Theater?
   a. It is very popular. The company performed nearly every day this month.
   b. It is very popular. All of its performances were sold out.
   c. It is not very popular. The company performed only in these four states.
   d. It is not very popular. It did not perform in large cities, such as New York and Chicago.

8. Do you think young people should attend performances of this dance company? Explain your answer.

EXPLORE MORE

Write a Report

Research information about the Alvin Ailey American Dance Theater since its founding in 1958 with Alvin and the eight black dancers he hired. Prepare an oral or written report that tells such information as how many members are in the theater today and how performances have changed since the beginning.

Be Artistic

Choose one of the mediums that Sheila Hamanaka enjoys and create an original piece of artwork. Describe what Sheila probably would like best about your creation.

Be a Sculptor

Collect a variety of objects you find just lying around, much as Louise Nevelson did. When you have a good collection, use them to create a piece of art. It could be a sculpture made by arranging the pieces in a certain way and gluing them together. Or it could be an arrangement on a flat piece of heavy paper. Ask your teacher to help you display your work.

Choose an Artist

Research one of the artists in this unit or another artist of your choosing, and prepare a written, oral, or visual presentation on the artist and his or her most popular works. Include any special conditions or circumstances the artist may have had to overcome in order to achieve artistic success.

Dance!

With a partner or small group— or by yourself—select a piece of music and choreograph a dance. Practice the dance several times. When you are ready, perform the dance for the rest of the class.

Visit a Museum

With a parent or other caregiver, visit an art museum in your area. Decide which is your favorite display or piece of art. If possible, take a photograph of the art. Then write a short description of your visit and of the art you selected. Tell who the artist was, how he or she created the piece, and why you think it's special.

Related Books

Bray-Moffatt, Naia. *Ballet School*. DK Publishing, 2003.

Cain, Michael. *Louise Nevelson*. Chelsea House Publishers, 1989.

Cummings, Pat. *Talking With Artists: Volume Two*. Simon & Schuster Books for Young Readers, 1995.

Dowd, Olympia. *On Tour With the Moscow City Ballet: A Young Dancer's Apprenticeship*. Twenty-First Century Books, 2003.

Fleming, Robert. *Alvin Ailey*. Holloway House Publishing Co., 2002.

Hegel, Claudette. *Newbery and Caldecott Trivia and More for Every Day of the Year*. Libraries Unlimited, Inc., 2000.

Kuklin, Susan. *Reaching for Dreams: A Ballet From Rehearsal to Opening Night*. Harry N. Abrams Publishing, 2001.

Lewis-Ferguson, Julinda. *Alvin Ailey, Jr.: A Life in Dance*. Walker and Company, 1994.

Marcus, Leonard S. *A Caldecott Celebration: Six Artists and Their Paths to the Caldecott Medal*. Walker and Co., 1998.

Nevelson, Louise. *Louise Nevelson: Sculpture & Collages, October 1— October 30, 1999*. Locks Gallery, 1999.

Pace Gallery Publishing Staff. *Louise Nevelson, Cascades, Perpendiculars, Silence, Music*. Pace Gallery Publications, 1983.

Pinkney, Andrea Davis. *Alvin Ailey*. Hyperion Books for Children, 1993.

Tobey, Cheryl. *Modern Dance*. Children's Press, 2001.

Interesting Web Sites

http://www.alvinailey.org
http://www.pbs.org/wnet/gperf/alvinailey/html/artists.html
http://texas-on-line.com/graphic/alvinailey.htm
http://www.culturevulture.net/Dance/Ailey.htm
http://www.alvinailey.org/history.asp?nav=1
http://www.americandancefestival.org/Archives/scripps/ailey.html
http://www.ala.org/alsc/caldecott.html
http://encarta.msn.com/encnet/refpages/refarticle.aspx?refid=761579641
http://www.randolphcaldecott.org.uk/who.htm
http://www.dailycelebrations.com/121999.htm
http://www.nmwa.org/collection/profile.asp?LinkID-633
http://www.niagara.edu/cam/collections/sculp.nevelson.html
http://usembassy.state.gov/tokyo/wwwhnevelson.html